"You've Always Thought of Yourself as a Dancer, Disregarding the Woman.

You just have to start listening to the woman in you."

Her heart was beating loudly, the blood pounding through her body as though she were in an echo chamber. She pulled back. "It's not that simple. . . ."

His arms encircled her as his mouth met hers, no longer gentle but demanding, passionately aggressive. He took her back in time, and she felt the excitement she knew before a performance and the exhilaration of the applause when she had danced her best.

"I want to make love to you, Lydia. I want to show you how much of a woman you are without your dancing. Stay with me tonight. Wake up with me tomorrow."

MARGARET RIPY
loves to travel and only writes about places she has visited. In her books there is a "little bit of herself and her experiences." Without the support and love of Mike, her husband of fourteen years, she says her writing wouldn't be possible. He has the characteristics she wants in a male hero.

Dear Reader:

Romance readers have been enthusiastic about Silhouette Special Editions for years. And that's not by accident: Special Editions were the first of their kind and continue to feature realistic stories with heightened romantic tension.

The longer stories, sophisticated style, greater sensual detail and variety that made Special Editions popular are the same elements that will make you want to read book after book.

We hope that you enjoy this Special Edition today, and will enjoy many more.

The Editors at Silhouette Books

MARGARET RIPY
Promise Her Tomorrow

Silhouette Special Edition
Published by Silhouette Books New York
America's Publisher of Contemporary Romance

To my son,
Shaun, with love

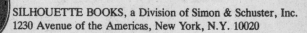

SILHOUETTE BOOKS, a Division of Simon & Schuster, Inc.
1230 Avenue of the Americas, New York, N.Y. 10020

Copyright © 1984 by Margaret Ripy
Cover artwork copyright © 1984 Herb Tauss

Distributed by Pocket Books

ISBN: 0-671-53709-1

First Silhouette Books printing December, 1984

10 9 8 7 6 5 4 3 2 1

Map by Ray Lundgren

SILHOUETTE, SILHOUETTE SPECIAL EDITION and
colophon are registered trademarks of Simon & Schuster, Inc.

America's Publisher of Contemporary Romance

Printed in the U.S.A.

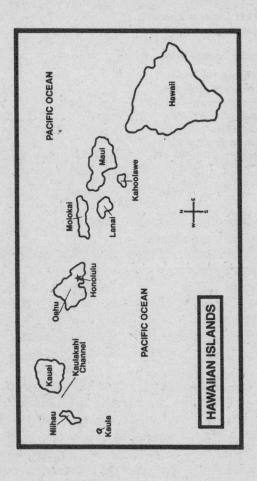

HAWAIIAN ISLANDS

Chapter One

Steven Winters neatly stacked the last folder he would need into his briefcase, then closed it, the lock clicking into place. Lifting his cool gray eyes a fraction, he scanned his desk to make sure he hadn't forgotten anything important for his trip. But as usual there was nothing. He was too thorough to forget something important, even a small detail, that had to do with Wintercom.

For just a moment he would permit himself the luxury of sitting down and finishing his lukewarm cup of coffee. He would need the caffeine; he planned to work most of the way to London on his new project for the company. The meetings, first in London then later in Paris and Munich, were essential to this latest project . . . his baby.

After finishing the last of his coffee, Steven inhaled

deeply, then released the breath on a sigh. He would be gone from the office for nearly a month, but even in Europe he planned to keep close tabs on the day-to-day decisions at Wintercom. Eric, his brother and new vice president, had a long way to go before he could take over efficiently for any length of time.

The sound of the door opening drew Steven's full attention to the man entering his office. Eric stood in the doorway a few seconds longer than necessary, appraising Steven with a wary look as though he were sizing up his opponent before a battle. The expression on his brother's face sparked a subtle tension that always sprang up instantly between them.

Steven tensed inwardly; outwardly he remained calm. For a fleeting moment he wondered if his brother and he would ever see eye to eye on anything. Where had their relationship gone wrong? he asked himself, not for the first time.

"So, you couldn't leave for a few weeks and give me any real authority." Eric closed the door, advanced into the spacious office, and came to a halt in front of Steven's desk. Eric leaned forward, his palms resting flat on the highly polished surface. "I shouldn't be surprised, brother dear. I'm just a token vice president anyway."

"Are you trying to induce my pity?" Steven drawled sarcastically. *Here we go again*, he thought wearily. *The line has been drawn.*

"Pity? From you? Never! That word isn't in your vocabulary." Eric straightened, a cocky grin sliding across his features. "Besides, if you ever decided to put me to work, when would I have time to play? Which brings me to the subject of why I came in here."

Steven arched a thick, dark eyebrow. "How much do you need this time?"

A slight tensing of Eric's shoulders was the only sign of his inner anger. The rakish grin was still plastered all over his face as he fitted his hands into his trouser pockets. "Will you be back in time for Mother's birthday? We're planning a big celebration for her sixtieth birthday next weekend."

"You know I won't be." Steven glanced at his gold wristwatch, then stood. "In fact, if I don't leave now, I'll be late for my plane."

"She wants you there," Eric said, the grin gone, replaced with a piercing regard. "You missed her last birthday. That's always an important day to Mother."

"I'll make it up to her when I get back. If I can finalize the deals while in Europe, within the year our pharmaceutical division will have plants in three European countries. That's important to Wintercom, therefore the family."

"No doubt the profits will go toward the research division of Wintercom. That division is more important to you than your family. In fact, making money is more important."

"You don't seem to turn down the money from the company." Picking up his briefcase, Steven pinned Eric beneath his penetrating, cool eyes like the clouds of a gathering storm. "As much as I'm enjoying this brotherly chat, I have to leave. I'll call Mother on her birthday."

"I'll take a couple hundred before you leave."

Flicking his brother an irritated glance, Steven placed his briefcase on the desk, withdrew his checkbook, and quickly wrote Eric a check. "Try to make that hold you until next week when you get your paycheck." He flipped the check toward Eric, the blue piece of paper floating down onto the desk top.

Without another word Steven retrieved his briefcase and strode toward the double doors. A sudden weariness claimed him as he opened the door. It was only two in the afternoon, but he had been at the office since five that morning, working nonstop. And he still had hours of work ahead of him.

Tyler Jackson half sat, half leaned against Steven's secretary's desk, laughing at something that she had said. For a few seconds Steven paused in the doorway, wishing he could relax and enjoy life like his friend. But there was always something he had to see to that demanded his time.

Listen to what your doctor says, Winters. You can't keep up this pace.

Banishing those uncharacteristic thoughts from his mind, Steven simply wouldn't allow the exhaustion to take hold. He had existed on far less sleep before and at the moment he couldn't afford—Wintercom couldn't afford for him—to take a vacation nor to slow down. *Maybe after Europe,* he thought.

"Ready," Steven said as he crossed the outer office toward his private elevator, his long strides purposeful now.

Tyler pushed off the desk, murmured good-bye to Steven's secretary, then followed Steven onto the elevator. "I see you've been at it again without bothering to get much sleep. Did you even go home last night?"

Steven laughed. "Do I look that bad?"

"No, I just know you and your work habits."

Punching the button for the garage, Steven grinned

wryly. "I don't know why I even bothered. I didn't sleep more than four restless hours. I finally gave up and came back into the office."

They stepped off the elevator and headed for Steven's white Lotus. The sports car was the one whim he had allowed himself the past year. He loved the feel of power it exuded. He had learned long ago that people didn't push you around or step on you if you had power. He swore when his father died that he wouldn't end up like him, a broken man near the point of bankruptcy, boxed into a corner by his competitors.

"Is everything tied up?" Tyler asked, having to quicken his pace to keep up with Steven.

"Everything is except that mess in Alabama."

Tyler opened the passenger's door, peering at Steven over the top of the sports car. "Why aren't you flying over in the company jet?"

"It's in California. An emergency came up and it will be tied up for a few more days." Steven didn't explain further, because he never told anyone more than he had to know. He was a very private person, because he had learned that if people didn't know him well, they were never quite sure how to handle him.

Steven climbed into the Lotus and fitted his long length into the small confines of the driver's seat. As he started the engine he looked sideways at his friend, amusement lurking in his gray eyes for a few seconds before saying, "And it won't work, Tyler. I want to discuss your negotiations concerning the C. P. Fielding Corporation down in Alabama. I want that company but not at the price the old man is asking and you're willing to pay." He pulled out into the heavy Manhattan traffic, heading his car toward Kennedy Airport.

"What do you consider a fair price?" A touch of anger, mixed with defensiveness, edged Tyler's words.

"Not what you've tentatively agreed upon." Everything about Steven was very controlled and quietly authoritative. The steely determination that made him one of the most feared men on Wall Street was evident, though, in his voice. "What's going on? I've never felt the need to oversee an acquisition before when you've been in charge. You're the best lawyer Wintercom has and a good friend." He pointedly looked at Tyler. "Why now?"

"Wintercom isn't being cheated."

"Don't kid me. I've known you too long. You're evading my question."

Tyler's jaw set stubbornly. "I don't know. I really thought the price was fair. The C. P. Fielding Corporation has great potential—"

"When it's managed correctly." Steven glanced at Tyler, then returned his attention to the traffic.

"Okay. Okay." Tyler's suppressed anger was surfacing rapidly. "His company did well up until a year ago when Fielding became ill and let the management become slack. Something you would never do, so I'm sure it's hard for you to understand."

"Don't make me out to be a villain in this deal, Tyler. I'm not out to steal his company." Steven paused, his controlled emotions held tightly reined. "It's Fielding's daughter, isn't it?" he asked in a quiet voice, looking again at Tyler.

Lydia Masters stuffed her toe shoes into her nylon bag, then started for the front door. *I'm late,* she thought, *and Anthony's going to have my head.*

The phone rang and Lydia stopped, glancing back at the coffee table where it sat. She started again for the door, but the persistent ringing drew her back toward the phone; she couldn't stand not knowing who was on the other end.

"Oh, thank God, I caught you before you left for the theater," the voice rushed as soon as she picked up the receiver. "They said you hadn't arrived yet for dress rehearsal."

Her brother sounded strained, and instantly Lydia became alert. Jason had lost his wife six months before and things hadn't been easy for him or his daughter.

"What's wrong, Jason?" Lydia swung her bag off her shoulder and placed it on the table as she sat on the couch.

"It's Maggie. I don't know what I'm going to do, Lydia. Mrs. Ford just called and told me that Maggie's school thinks she should be taken out of regular first grade. I'm wrapping up my commitments here as fast as I can, so I'll be able to spend some time with her. Will you go out to Connecticut to speak with Mrs. Ford, and visit with Maggie for a while?"

Lydia bit into her lower lip, a frown narrowing her green eyes. She wanted to tell her brother so many things, but she also knew his work, his singing, was the one thing that had held him together the past six months. But still, Maggie needed her father. "Jason, *you* should be doing those things."

"I know, Lydia," came the whispered reply. Jason cleared his throat, then continued in a stronger voice, "It's that house. Diana fell down the stairs there and ever since then it's been hard for me to go home. I'll be there next week. I promise, Sis. Please see about Maggie."

"You know I will. I'll go out on Sunday. It's my free day this week. Now, if I don't get going, Anthony's going to fire me and then I'd have too much free time." Rising, Lydia slung her dance bag over her shoulder.

"How could he do that? You're his star. You're one of the best ballet dancers in the world."

Lydia blushed. She had never been able to accept compliments well. "That's just my big brother talking."

"No, that's the media talking. I'll see you next week."

"Fine. Good-bye."

"And, Sis . . . thanks for being there."

Lydia quickly hung up the phone and hurried from her apartment, glancing at her watch as she descended the stairs. Dress rehearsal would be starting in thirty minutes and it was a good twenty-block walk downtown to Lincoln Center. For a brief moment she considered taking a cab but dismissed that thought. Spring had finally arrived and the weather was gorgeous, the first time in months. She would put up with Anthony's ranting and raving because the fresh air would be worth it. Besides, she needed some time to put the problem with her niece in perspective.

Maggie's so withdrawn, Lydia thought as she remembered seeing her niece two weeks before. The whole time she had been at her brother's house Maggie hadn't said one word. She hadn't spoken more than a few sentences since her mother's freak accident. It was so unlike the Maggie Lydia had known before Diana's death.

Lydia crossed a side street, hurrying the last few

steps as the light changed and a taxi sped across the intersection.

But then, Maggie had been through so much, having witnessed her mother's fall. Lydia shivered even now as she recalled Mrs. Ford's account. The housekeeper had heard Maggie's screams and had rushed from the kitchen to find Diana at the bottom of the stairs. Maggie was hugging her mother and begging her to get up. After that Maggie withdrew totally into her own world, never shedding a tear for her mother.

I could throttle Jason. He can be so insensitive at times. Doesn't he realize Maggie's hurting as much, maybe more, than he?

Looking again at her watch, Lydia hurried her pace and decided to take a short cut to the center. In the middle of the street she stepped off the curb between two parked cars and started to cross. As she glanced up she saw a white sports car coming toward her and for an instant she was paralyzed.

Tyler stared sharply at Steven, whose profile was carved with an iron hand. "I'm interested in Nancy, but I honestly didn't think our relationship was interfering with business. I just don't agree with you on this, Steven."

"Sometimes, Tyler, you're a soft touch. Not often, thank God." A smile in Steven's eyes as his attention strayed momentarily to Tyler took the sting out of the rebuke. "I know it's been hard for you after your divorce."

"You're damn right it has. I'm not like you, Steven. I don't like living alone, with my work being my only companion. I need more than that."

Something in Tyler's words cut deep into Steven and his grip on the steering wheel tightened. Steven started to speak, to get the conversation back on business, when he saw the woman in the road. He slammed his foot onto the brake pedal, his hold on the steering wheel deadly tight, his muscles locking as he tried to swerve to miss the woman.

The bumping sound jarred Steven, and a cold sweat blanketed him in an icy sheath. Seconds later, which seemed like hours, the car came to a halt, turned sideways in the street. Steven pried his fingers off the steering wheel, fighting desperately for the control he was noted for. In the second he had glimpsed the woman in the street, all he could remember was the panic on her face, her eyes huge, her body rigid with fear.

Oh, my God, what have I done?

His hand trembled as he reached for the door handle. The battle for control lasted only a brief moment before it fell into place and Steven was out of his car and rounding the front of it. A small crowd was forming which Tyler, joining Steven, pushed back.

Sitting on his haunches, Steven felt at the woman's neck for a pulse. *She's alive!* But the pulse was rapid and weak.

"Call an ambulance, Tyler. Quick."

Steven didn't want to risk moving her, but he did take off his suit coat and lay it over her, his gaze traveling down her slim body, clad in jeans, until it rested upon her left leg, twisted oddly, a bone at her ankle sticking out. He shut his eyes against the sight. His wheel must have caught her there.

With his heartbeat thumping rapidly against his

chest, he fought down the nausea churning in his stomach and ran his gaze up her body to her face. For the first time, he saw the beauty in the woman's delicate features. Fleetingly he thought he knew this woman, but surely if he had met her, he would remember that haunting face.

Her eyes drifted open and stared blankly into his face for a few seconds before her eyelids fluttered, then closed. Steven sucked in deep breaths. Those startlingly green eyes, accusing and unforgiving, had branded him guilty.

Steven hadn't even realized that Tyler had returned until his friend laid a hand on his arm and said, "The police are here, Steven. The ambulance is on its way."

Steven stood and answered the policeman's questions, giving the officer all the information he needed from him to fill out the accident report. But all the while Steven was talking, his gaze was riveted on the attendants, who had arrived moments before and were preparing to transport the woman to the hospital. Several times the policeman had to repeat a question because Steven couldn't rid his thoughts of the mushrooming guilt that was eating away at him. Her left leg, with its prominent odd twist, couldn't be dismissed. He felt his life for once was totally slipping out of his control.

The attendants were placing the woman into the ambulance as the officer finished his questioning. Steven turned to Tyler and said, "I'm going with her to the hospital. Take care of everything else here for me." He tossed the last sentence over his shoulder as he walked toward the ambulance.

"I'm riding with you to the hospital."

The unyielding tone in Steven's voice caused the attendant to look up at him. "Are you a relative?"

"A friend—a *good* friend," Steven lied.

The attendant shrugged. "Okay." His knowing regard clearly conveyed what kind of friend he thought Steven was.

But Steven didn't care how he was able to ride in the ambulance as long as he did. He climbed in behind the attendant, the sound of the closing door reverberating through his mind as though part of his life was all of a sudden shut off from him. On the ride to the hospital, he tried to shake the feeling of overwhelming helplessness, but he couldn't.

At the hospital the woman was whisked away into an emergency room, still unconscious. Steven began the waiting, pacing back and forth in the small room where the nurse had directed him.

When Tyler arrived, Steven noticed that his friend's face was pale, concern in his expression. Tyler handed him a cup of coffee, which he gladly took. He downed the warm brew in several swallows, then began his restless prowling again.

"I know what you're thinking, Steven."

Steven halted and turned toward his friend. "Do you?" He took a pack of cigarettes from his coat pocket and shook one out. He lit it, inhaled deeply, then blew a ring of smoke out, none of his tension dissipating. It was coiled about him like a boa constrictor squeezing tighter and tighter as the minutes passed and no one came to tell him if she would be all right.

"You're feeling responsible for the accident." Tyler

squarely faced Steven, his next words spoken very slowly to allow each one to sink in. "The accident was not your fault. She stepped out in front of your car in the middle of the street."

Crushing his cigarette out in an ashtray, Steven combed his fingers through his neatly trimmed black hair, a gesture of frustration that he rarely made. "Does it really make any difference whose fault it is right now? There's a woman in that room over there who was hit by *my* car."

"It makes a world of difference, Steven, legally."

"The hell with legality. Did you see her left leg?" The usual quiet in his voice rose several levels.

"There's something else you'd better know."

Steven froze at the uneasy tone in his friend's voice.

"The woman is Lydia Masters."

Lydia Masters! Who wouldn't know that name. *Her injured leg.* Again he relived in his mind the jarring impact of metal hitting flesh and bones. He was numb, as if delayed shock had finally set in.

"There isn't anything you can do here, Steven. But those meetings in Europe are vital to Wintercom's future. You need them if you want to push ahead on your project. I'll take care of everything here. When I came in, I checked with the nurse on duty. They're going to take her up to surgery in a few minutes to repair her leg."

"I can't leave, Tyler," Steven replied in a monotone. Again he saw the frightened horror on her face the instant she had known she wouldn't escape being hit. He shut his eyes and shook his head violently.

"What are you going to do here? What good will it

do to sit in a waiting room for a report? I'll stay and let you know her progress. She will make it, Steven."

Why now? Why me? Suddenly Steven was the frightened one.

"I want to pay all her bills—everything, Tyler. I want you to see to it personally."

"Okay, but you don't have to pay the bills."

"Yes, I do. And I want you to keep me posted on what's going on." Steven hesitated, his glance pulled to the emergency room door that Lydia Masters had disappeared behind.

"Fine." Tyler touched Steven's arm, nudging him toward the door. "I've already changed your flight reservation to a later one. You have only an hour and a half to make it, so you'd better leave now."

"Yeah," Steven said absently, his attention still upon the closed door. He had no right to stay there. He would be the intruder.

"Come on." Tyler handed Steven his piece of luggage and briefcase. "There isn't a thing you can do for her now. It's out of your hands. Remember, there wasn't anything you could do to prevent that accident."

"Tell that to Lydia Masters." Steven turned away and headed for the door.

He had been to the ballet several times and had seen Lydia Masters dance twice. Each time he had walked away knowing he had witnessed a unique beauty, rare and precious. She had spoken with her body as if she had known no other form of communication to express her passion for life and the depth of her emotions. Each gesture and movement of hers had been an effortless extension of the one before.

Steven couldn't help but wonder what Lydia Masters would have left after this accident. For the first time in his life he felt like running scared. Why else would he have permitted Tyler to talk him into leaving so easily for his business trip as planned? No one ever talked him into anything.

Chapter Two

Lydia desperately clung to the black restful void for as long as possible. Each time she moved toward consciousness she felt the inevitable throbbing pain and quickly sought refuge in the deep dreamless sleep. She was used to pain and aches but this was different.

Slowly her eyes half opened. Her mouth was parched; her lips were dry. She ran her tongue over her lips. Suddenly, the image of her brother came into view. Her eyes opened completely, and she stared into Jason's concerned regard.

His half grin was crooked, forced as he said, "I thought you would never wake up. When we were kids you were the first one up and you always managed to wake up everyone else within five minutes."

Her mind was cloudy, her thoughts scattered in a hundred different directions. She blinked, licking her lips again. Shifting slightly in the bed, she was instantly aware of the pain that sharpened intensely with the movement. Every muscle ached as if she had danced for twenty-four hours straight.

"Water," she finally rasped.

Jason reached for the pitcher on the bedside table and poured the water into a plastic glass. The one thing Lydia noticed was that her brother's hands were trembling. She drank the water, her attention intently upon her brother's face.

There were so many questions she wanted to ask, but it took too much effort to speak. Instead, Lydia drifted back into a deep sleep.

Jason sat for a long time staring at his sister in the hospital bed, taking in deep breaths to still the pounding of his heart. He didn't know what he was going to say to her when she awakened again.

He stood and walked to the window that looked down upon the busy street below. Jamming his hands into the pockets of his pants, his body stiff, his eyes stinging from lack of sleep, he leaned his forehead against the cool windowpane. Lydia's whole life was her dancing, since the age of five. *Now I will have to tell her that at twenty-nine she will have to start over and find something else to do.*

His hands, clenched into tight fists, stretched the confines of his pockets. Even though she was his younger sister, he had felt at times, especially lately, that Lydia was the stronger of the two. She had been his Rock of Gibraltar when Diana had died, always there when he needed her even though her schedule was as busy as his own.

For a long time Jason stood at the window as dark gray clouds moved in and it began to rain. His mind sank deeper into a depression as rivulets of water streaked the windowpane.

"Jason."

He whirled around at the faint sound of his name and stared at Lydia, who was wide awake, her eyes glued to the cast below her elbow on her right arm.

"Jason!" Hysterics laced her voice as her gaze shifted to the cast on her left leg.

Quickly he rushed to the bed and took her hand within his as he sat down next to her. "Hello, Sis."

"My arm. My leg!" Her voice was becoming stronger, her eyes rounder. They never veered from the cast on her leg, covered by a sheet but still very obvious. "What's wrong?" She swallowed hard, again and again trying to coat her dry throat but nothing helped. "What's wrong, Jason?" Lydia repeated, her full attention suddenly flying to his face.

He frantically searched for a painless way to tell his sister that she would never be able to do the one thing she loved the most, to dance. But there was no painless way.

"Tell me, Jason!" she demanded, watching the play of emotions parade across his face. Her alarm soared as he discarded one expression after another until finally a deep sadness settled in his hazel eyes.

Jason looked down at their clasped hands as he started to speak. No words would come. With eyes misting, he finally answered, "Your left ankle has multiple fractures and the doctors had to pin it. You'll never be able to dance again, Lydia."

Her tight grip on his hand slackened. "Never dance

again," she repeated in a whisper. "No, you're wrong, Jason. You have to be!"

With a violent shake of her head she denied her brother's words, the movement producing a sharp pain at the base of her skull. She groaned and shut her eyes against the spinning room.

"Please, take it easy, Lydia. You also have internal injuries that will take time to heal." Jason wrapped his fingers securely around her hand, trying to transmit his concern, love, and strength. He'd give anything to be able to turn back the clock. "I wish I were wrong. As it is, it will be months before you'll walk again. Because of your fractured wrist, you'll be in a wheelchair for several months until it's healed and you're strong enough to use crutches."

Lydia swung her gaze back to the cast on her arm. She pulled her hand free from Jason's clasp and touched the cast in slow motion as though she were afraid she would burn herself. As she fingered it lightly the green of her eyes darkened.

She closed her eyes and wished she had never awakened. She felt so numb, as if she were dreaming, and that at any moment she would wake up and be at the dress rehearsal. But the dull pain quickly sobered her, making it vividly clear that this was no nightmare but real life.

"Lydia?"

She opened her eyes but stared straight ahead. "The doctor could be wrong. I want a second opinion."

"I had three doctors look at you. They all agreed. Lydia, you know in your heart they're right. How could you dance on toes with an ankle that will always be weak?"

She wanted to cry so badly, but it was as though her emotions were frozen in a block of ice. "Why me, Jason? Why?" All she saw was the stark white sheet stretched out over her legs, reminding her of the sudden bleakness of her life. And like the sterile decor of the hospital room, her life would be barren without dance.

Jason clasped her hand again tightly. "I can't answer that. I couldn't answer that question six months ago when Diana died." His voice was ragged with painful memories.

Her heart felt like it was expanding to choke off her next breath. The walls of the room seemed to be closing in on her. *You'll never dance again*. Her temples were throbbing with a razor-sharp tension. The weight of the future pressed down upon her.

All she wanted to do was sleep—all the way through the next few months. As her eyelids slowly lowered she murmured, "Please don't leave me, Jason. I'm scared."

Even before opening her eyes, Lydia tried to move her left leg, but the cast weighted it down, the dull ache intensifying whenever she shifted. She touched her arm cast and its cold reality canceled out any hope that she had been living a dream.

When she opened her eyes, Jason was sitting next to her in a chair, hunched over with his arms folded on the bed and his head resting on top of them. He must have sensed her awakening because he lifted his head and looked up. Lydia gasped at the disheveled appearance of her brother, unshaven, his brown hair unruly.

"How long have you been here?" Lydia asked,

running her fingers through his hair, trying to bring some kind of order to it.

"For a couple of days. I didn't want to leave. I knew I had to be the one to tell you the truth. We've been through so much, Sis, I couldn't let a stranger do it." Straightening, Jason stretched, then rubbed his reddened eyes.

"Have you even bothered to sleep?" At the moment it was easier to focus on her brother than herself.

"Not much. I think the nurses were about ready to carry me out bodily."

"Have you seen Maggie?"

"No. When Mom called with the news, I came straight here from Las Vegas. Mom wanted to come up but I told her I would take care of everything. She can't leave Dad yet. He still has a long way to go recovering from his stroke. This last year has sure been hell for the Masters family." Bitterness edged his voice.

"Does—does anyone know . . ." Her voice faltered and she couldn't complete her question.

But Jason knew what Lydia meant. "No, not yet. I haven't even told Mom and Dad, Lydia. What do you want me to do?"

"I don't want anyone to know," she said without thinking.

"Mom and Dad have a right to know the extent of your injuries and so does Anthony. He's been here several times along with a dozen dancers from the company. You can't keep this a secret. Too many people are concerned for you, Lydia." Jason paused, uncertain whether to mention the lawyer. "And Tyler Jackson has been here most of the time."

"Tyler Jackson? I don't know anyone by that name."

Jason's gaze dropped to his lap. "He's the lawyer of the man who was driving the car that hit you."

"Lawyer? His client is really quick," Lydia said sarcastically.

"You don't have to see the man. I can handle it."

"No! I want to see him. I'm sure this is the closest I will get to the man responsible for this." Lydia gestured toward her casts.

Her shock had receded, and she knew the only thing left was to face the fact she wouldn't be able to dance. Lesser injuries than a multiple fracture disabled a dancer, making it impossible to perform again. She hated self-pity but was having a difficult time keeping it at bay. Turning her anger toward the man behind the wheel was easier than feeling sorry for herself.

When Jason sagged back in the chair, closing his eyes, Lydia said, "Go home, Jason. Maggie needs her father. You need some sleep."

"Will you be all right?"

She wanted to shout, "No, never again without my dancing," but instead she answered with a short laugh. "Yes, of course. I'm not going anywhere. I'll still be here when you've rested and seen Maggie."

But Jason didn't laugh. "I know when you're hurting the most, you try to make light of it. I'll be back tomorrow morning, in better shape I hope." He rose, leaned over, and kissed her on the cheek.

After Jason left the hospital room, the silence became unbearable; she began to think about her future. What future? She didn't know anything except dancing. It had been her job, her hobby, her love for almost twenty-five years.

She closed her eyes, desperately wanting to escape into the world of sleep, but instead, a picture of the accident flashed into her mind. She was standing motionless in the street, watching the white sports car bearing down on her, unable to move even an inch. No! Her eyes flew open, focusing again on the sterile hospital room. Shaking, she raised a hand to her forehead.

"Good afternoon, Lydia." The dance company's doctor suddenly walked into the room. "I spoke with Jason and he told me you knew."

It took a moment for her to speak. She felt so cold, yet her hands were sweaty. "Yes, Dr. Daly," she finally said. "Have you come to tell me he was wrong?"

"No. I'm here to check up on you and to answer any questions you might have." The doctor examined her, not saying a word, his expression neutral. "Any questions, Lydia?"

"What is the extent of my injuries? I want to know everything."

"You have a multiple fractured left ankle that might require several operations to fix. You have a fracture of the right wrist. And you also have internal injuries, a mild concussion and an assortment of bruises and scrapes that will heal in no time."

As Dr. Daly continued to talk Lydia felt as though nails were being placed in a coffin containing her dreams and hopes, and with each word the nails were being pounded deeper and deeper into the wood, sealing her fate.

"And after the operations on my leg, what then?"

"You'll begin to learn to walk again."

For a moment Lydia's teeth were clamped so tightly

together that a sharp pain shot down her neck. "I know how to walk, Dr. Daly."

"By the time you're out of that wheelchair and the cast is off your leg, it will be almost three months from now. Your muscles will have to be conditioned again. Of anyone, you should know how easy it is for a muscle to lose its strength. Just think—all you'll be doing for weeks is lying in bed or sitting in a chair."

"Why can't I have a walking cast when I leave the hospital? Why a wheelchair?" She emphasized *wheelchair* as though she was appalled to have to even mention such a word.

"In its present condition your ankle can't bear the weight, Lydia. When your wrist is healed, you can use crutches."

She dreaded asking the next question but she had to know. "How much trouble will my ankle be after the therapy and I learn to walk again?"

"It will remind you from time to time that it's been broken. It might swell or ache. For a while you'll probably walk with a limp, but you'll be able to do most everyday activities."

"All the things I don't really care about. Thank you, Dr. Daly."

Looking away, Lydia didn't see him leave, but she heard the door close. She stared out the window at the rain striking against the glass pane. It sounded like someone with long fingernails scratching to get in. She concentrated on the sound of the falling raindrops, turning her thoughts away from what Dr. Daly had told her. There would be plenty of time in the future to deal with all the problems she had to face. Right now she was exhausted and wished she could wipe her mind clean of everything, past, present and future. Then she wouldn't feel this vast emptiness inside her.

"Lydia, may we come in," a deep baritone voice called from the doorway.

Lydia twisted her head around and watched as Anthony and Dora entered. Anthony was carrying a large bouquet of red and white roses, their potent fragrance suffusing the room. Dora wore jeans over her tights and leotard; Lydia knew that she had come directly from the morning class and would have to go back to the theater soon for a rehearsal. The sight of her friend in dancing attire shattered Lydia's fragile control, which she struggled to retain in front of her two colleagues. She didn't want anyone's pity, especially Anthony and Dora's. But Lydia suddenly felt a line being drawn between her friends and herself and she would never be allowed to cross over again into their world.

The corners of Lydia's mouth barely turned upward as she raised her hand to take Anthony's in welcome. She saw the emotions that he was fighting to suppress; he couldn't mask the pity that was deep in his eyes. No one had told him that she couldn't dance on the stage again, but Lydia knew he didn't have to be told.

Anthony brushed his lips across Lydia's. "How's my ballerina doing?" His forced smile wavered as he straightened and Dora stepped closer to the bed.

"Doing cartwheels down the hall," Lydia quipped. She hadn't meant to sound cynical, but that was the way it had come out.

The air thickened with strained tension as Dora and Anthony glanced at each other.

Lydia looked away from her friends, but she felt their

gazes on her, intently sympathetic. "I'm sorry. It didn't come out the way I meant it."

Anthony cleared his throat, then asked gently, "How long will you be in the hospital? The doctor wouldn't tell us anything. And Jason's gone home."

"I'm not sure." Lydia turned back to look straight into Anthony's eyes. "I won't ever dance again, Anthony. My left ankle is useless." She waved her hand toward the cast. She made sure her expression showed none of the disgust she was feeling. Then because she had to or else lose all control, Lydia changed the subject and asked, "How did opening night go?"

"Oh, great!" Dora automatically answered in her enthusiastic voice, then caught herself before continuing in a more sedate tone, "I mean, everyone missed you, but the audience was"—she searched for the right word—"responsive."

"Well, I was slightly delayed crossing the street. You know New York traffic can be horrid at times." There she went again, trying to make light of a situation that was tearing her apart inside.

"Anthony, I'll be outside," Dora murmured, then quietly left, looking back once before closing the door.

"I'm sorry. I didn't mean to run her off."

"Quit apologizing for everything you say, Lydia." Anthony threw his hands up in the air. "You have a right to be angry as hell." He sat in the chair by the bed. "Dora doesn't always think before she speaks."

"But she is a friend and I shouldn't have said that."

"I would have said a lot more if I had been you." He scanned the room as if the decor suddenly interested him a great deal. "No one would tell me anything over the phone except that you were finally awake. I didn't realize . . ." His words faded as he groped for the right thing to say.

"You can say it. I've accepted it."

He pinned her beneath a shrewdly sharp look. "Have you, Lydia? I wouldn't have and I doubt seriously that you have. I wish there was a magical word to say to you that would help ease the pain. But there isn't. There will always be a place for you in the company. If not dancing, then choreographing or teaching."

"Don't throw me leftovers!"

"Damn it, I'm not." Anthony shot to his feet and walked to the window. He looked out for a moment as he tried to gather his composure, then finally he returned to the bedside. He towered over her, his powerful muscular frame filling her vision. "You have so much talent, such a rare gift. Why in God's name did it have to be you?" Tears crowded his eyes as he stared down at her. He collapsed into the chair, taking her hand within his large ones. "Oh, Lydia, I'm the one who's sorry. I didn't mean to come in here and say that. You don't need to hear that right now. Ever since I heard about your accident I couldn't shake the fear for you that I've been feeling. And then when no one would tell me anything. I . . ."

Painfully Lydia sat up and embraced Anthony, her throat tight with tears that she couldn't release and wanted to desperately. "I love you, Anthony. You've been my friend ever since I first joined the company. Ten years of friendship goes a long way in my book. You can say anything you want because I know it comes from someone who cares for me."

"Then please don't turn my offer down. You know I don't hand out leftovers. You have to earn everything you get in my company," he whispered close to her ear, his hand stroking the length of her back.

Lydia pulled away and collapsed against the pillow, that slight exertion tiring her more than a morning of classes. "I can't give you an answer now, Anthony. I'm so confused. I can hardly think about much of anything."

"I'm not pressing you for an answer, darling. When you're ready, think it over and let me know. Just remember you have a lot to offer the company and a lot to teach the young dancers."

Her first inclination was to say, "No! I can't bear to watch teenage dancers doing what I love to do." But maybe in time she would be able to live on the fringes of the ballet world and be able to cope with the change. She would eventually have to, anyway.

"I'll think about it, Anthony." She smiled faintly.

"Well, I have to get Dora back to the theater for the rehearsal of—" He stopped in mid-sentence.

"Don't be afraid to talk about ballet in front of me. I'm not made of fine china, Anthony. Dora is taking my part in *Sleeping Beauty*?"

He nodded.

"She'll be a good Aurora."

"I'll come by tomorrow." Anthony kissed her lightly, then left.

Not a minute after Anthony had gone the door opened again and a man of medium height walked into the room. A puzzled expression descended on Lydia's face as she watched the stranger advance toward the bed. Her first thought was that the man had the wrong room, then she remembered Jason talking about a lawyer who had wanted to see her. Her pulse began to race; her hands became clammy.

"Miss Masters, I'm Tyler Jackson. I represent Steven Winters, the man who was driving the car that hit you."

Steven Winters. She would never forget that name; it was forever burned into her memory.

"Even though Mr. Winters was not responsible for the accident, he would like to pay for your hospital bills."

When the lawyer stressed the words *not responsible* her face flushed with anger. "Why, if as you say Mr. Winters isn't responsible, does he want to pay my bills?" Her voice was icy, her look frosty.

Tyler shifted his weight and for a brief moment he looked uncomfortable. He didn't know how to answer the question so he replied, "He has his reasons."

"Well, Mr. Jackson, you may tell Mr. Winters for me, since he has sent you instead of coming personally, that I would never accept his charity. I do not want to have anything to do with him and frankly I'm glad he was smart enough not to come himself. I can take care of myself. Good day, Mr. Jackson."

Lydia turned her head away and stared at the far wall until the sound of the door closing filled the air. She released her pent-up breath on a long, heavy sigh. As she lifted her hand to brush her hair away from her face, it was shaking so much that she curled it into a tight fist to stop the trembling.

Steven Winters. Steven Winters! The name made her want to scream. Before, the driver had been nameless and faceless. Now she at least had a name to put to the man who had altered the course of her life.

Steven sat at the table in his suite, listening to the representative from the bank. This series of meetings would be his easiest ones so far this trip. He had been in London five days and was almost ready to conclude to his satisfaction the first deal for Wintercom. He should have been elated; he wasn't.

The phone ringing interrupted the meeting and Steven stood. "Excuse me, gentlemen. I'll be with you in a moment." He then answered the phone in the bedroom of the suite.

"Steven, this is Tyler."

Steven stiffened instantly. He had tried not to think about the situation in New York, and yet it had always been in the back of his mind, even during business meetings. Never before had he allowed anything to interfere with his concentration while conducting business.

"Have you talked with her?"

"Yes, a few hours ago at the hospital. Steven, she won't accept the money. In fact, she wants nothing to do with you."

"Pay the bills anyway," Steven ground out between clenched teeth.

"I don't think that would be a good idea."

"Why won't she take the money? It's free. I'm not attaching any strings to it."

"I suppose the lady means it when she says nothing."

"Then you go back and make her see that it's foolish to reject the offer. I have enough money and certainly won't miss it. She's a dancer and I don't care how good she was, she doesn't have money to throw away."

"Why, Steven?"

Steven didn't like being backed into a corner with no escape. "Just do it!"

In a resigned voice Tyler replied, "I'll do it, but I can tell you right now Lydia Masters means what she says. I think you've done all you can. If the lady doesn't want your money, then it's been taken out of your hands."

The hell it has! He didn't like things being taken out of his hands. Steven was a controller and he was determined to be in complete control of this situation.

"Pay the bill, Tyler," Steven replied quietly. "Let me know when you've talked with her again." He hesitated for several long seconds, then asked the inevitable question, "How bad is it?"

"Bad."

Steven's heartbeat slowed, his grip tightened on the receiver.

"I talked with her brother after I saw her. He didn't say much at first, but finally I managed to get the bare facts out of him when he blew up at me. She won't dance again. She'll be confined to a wheelchair for the next couple of months. She has a broken wrist and her ankle was fractured in several places. It might require a couple of operations to repair the ankle."

When Steven hung up the phone, he sank onto the bed, his hand still on the cold plastic. Confined to a wheelchair. A woman who had floated across a stage, dazzling an audience with the grace and power of her unusual ability. *And I did this to her.*

The hand on the phone slipped to his side, but still he

sat on the bed. He had kept telling himself over and over that the accident hadn't been his fault. But maybe if he hadn't been arguing with Tyler about the Fielding acquisition, he would have seen her step off the curb and been able to avoid the collision. Every time he relived the accident in his mind, he couldn't shake that heavy feeling of responsibility. It had been important for her to accept the money; it had been a way for him to handle his guilt. Now he didn't know what to do.

Slowly he rose and reentered the living room, apologizing to the three men for the delay. The representative from the bank picked up where he had left off. Steven heard the words the banker was saying, but they passed through his mind like sand through a sifter. Their meaning was lost to him as he found himself doodling on a pad the words *Lydia Masters* and *wheelchair*. He couldn't rid himself of the picture of her in a wheelchair.

He snapped the pencil he was holding in half. The stunned expressions on the three men's faces and the uneasy silence roused Steven and finally locked his undivided attention on the meeting at hand.

But when the men left the hotel suite an hour later, the haunting images returned to plague him. He fixed himself a whiskey and soda and downed the drink in two swallows. Studying the bottom of his empty glass, he tried to figure out what to do next, but for once he didn't have a ready answer.

Chapter Three

*L*ydia leaned over, opened the bedside table drawer, and withdrew a hand mirror and a makeup bag. She didn't wear a lot of makeup unless performing on stage, but lately in the hospital she found herself putting it on heavily at first to mask the bruises and scratches on her face. Now, however, it was to conceal the dark shadows under her dull eyes from lack of sleep and to add some color to her ashen features. But no amount of makeup would give her green eyes the sparkle they used to have. Anyone looking at her could read her thoughts, her emotions through her eyes. From years of dancing, she had always been a very expressive person, using her body language to communicate her feelings.

She painstakingly made up her face every morning. It helped bolster her spirits and gave her something to do. After she finished applying the last touch, a deep red blush, she appraised herself in the hand mirror. Turning the mirror away from her in disgust, she wished for the hundredth time that she could wear dark, dark sunglasses in the room.

I'm just going to have to become proficient at hiding my feelings, she declared to herself. It was the look in her eyes when people came to visit that heightened their pity. No matter how much she laughed, kidded them, and smiled, that look of raw pain was always there.

"Good morning, beautiful," Jason said from the doorway, interrupting her morose train of thought.

Lydia smiled and replaced her mirror and makeup bag in the drawer. The only person she looked forward to seeing was her brother.

"Maggie sends her love." Jason sat in the chair by the bed.

"She's talking to you again!"

Looking away, he murmured, "Well, no, not exactly. But you two were always close."

"Oh. Jason, does Maggie know you're leaving tomorrow for an engagement at Lake Tahoe?"

"Yes. This is my last one for a while, Lydia. I'm doing this for the man who gave me my big break in the business. I owe Rod."

"And your daughter?"

Jason frowned. "Don't you give me a lecture, too. Mom's already done it." He stared out the window for a few minutes, then back at Lydia. "Until I came home this last time, I didn't realize how bad it was with Maggie. I guess I've been running from the truth about my daughter. I've been wallowing so much in my own misery that I forgot about hers. She's started therapy and when I'm through with this gig, we're going on a long vacation together."

"She needs you most of all." Lydia threw up her arm, palm outward, when she saw him scowl. "That's the last word you'll hear from me today on the subject."

"Today, but what about tomorrow?"

"You won't be here," she retorted lightly.

"But there's always the phone, sister dear. You've never been one to keep quiet about much of anything. I will say, you certainly aren't one to keep everything bottled up inside of yourself."

"Must be the Irish blood."

"We don't have any," Jason said with a laugh.

"Then the Italian."

"None."

"Okay, then my passionate artistic nature." Her laughter rolled from her throat.

"I'll buy that." There was a full-fledged smile on his face now. "I haven't heard you laugh in a long time. It sounds wonderful."

"It feels good, too, Jason. For just a moment I forgot everything except for the way we have always liked to banter back and forth."

"I wish I could stay, Lydia." A serious note entered his voice.

"Believe it or not, I do understand. Sell the house, Jason. Have you considered that the house might have bad memories for Maggie, too? After all, she's the one who was with Diana when she fell."

Jason ran his fingers through his hair, then rubbed the back of his neck, carefully reflecting on her suggestion. "No, I hadn't. I didn't want to uproot Maggie any more than she already was by moving to another place. But you may be right. I'll think about that."

"How's Dad doing? When I talk with Mom on the phone, she's always very careful with what she says to me. Half the time I think she's keeping something bad from me."

"No, Dad's doing fine. Better every day. Are you going to a rehabilitation clinic for your physical therapy?"

Lydia had rejected the clinic when Dr. Daly had talked with her about her therapy. Ever since she was a child, when she was hurting inside, she sought solitude. She couldn't face being around other people at a clinic, and shook her head in answer.

"Then are you going home after you get out of the hospital, Lydia?"

"No," she answered immediately.

"Then you're going to stay in New York?"

"No," she answered just as quickly. "I'm not sure what I want to do except that I can't stay here, not so near the dance world and my friends. I don't think I could handle that and also learning to walk again."

"Then why not go home to Louisville?"

"Because you know how Mom smothers and fusses over us when we're sick. I don't want that either."

Jason's face brightened into a smile. "I've got just the answer for you. You can recuperate at my house on Kauai. It will be a great change of scenery for you and you can be as secluded as you want." A look of understanding crossed Jason's face. He knew her well; they were a lot alike.

Lydia tilted her head at an angle and thought for a moment, warming to the suggestion. "That might not be a bad idea after all. I could hire a physical therapist to live with me. It would be expensive but worth it."

"Good. Then it's all settled. You have a place to go. Later, after my gig, Maggie and I can fly over and spend some time with you." He held up his hand, an impish look on his face. "I promise that Maggie and I won't smother or fuss over you."

Lydia laughed.

Jason rose and kissed her. "See how good I am for you. You laughed twice today. I'll call before we show. See you in Hawaii."

Jason wasn't gone five minutes when the door opened again and Tyler Jackson entered the room. Tensing, Lydia marshaled her defenses about her and tried to disguise her anger behind a cold facade.

"I'm glad you could come, Mr. Jackson. I thought I would tell you in person so I could make sure you understand that what we discussed two weeks ago still stands." Lydia waited until she was sure she had Mr. Jackson's full attention. "The hospital informed me yesterday that you went ahead and arranged to pay my bills without my consent. I don't want Mr. Winters' blood money and it's your job to get that point across to the man. I'm capable of paying my own bills. I'm not a pauper, Mr. Jackson." With the last sentence her voice quavered slightly. Her anger was escalating out of control.

Tyler stood at the foot of the bed, a neutral expression on his face. "I'll tell Mr. Winters what you said, Miss Masters. But it would make things easier if you just took the money. Mr. Winters is a very determined man."

"Then he has met his match. A dancer doesn't get to

the top of her profession without a lot of determination, Mr. Jackson," she informed him in a crisp voice, her green eyes narrowing. "I don't want one penny of Mr. Winters' money. Not a penny, do you understand?"

Tyler nodded his head, his jaw set in a grim line.

"Thank you for coming, Mr. Jackson, on such short notice. Good day." She dismissed him with her cool voice.

"Good day, Miss Masters." He paused while turning away. "I'm sorry for everything."

"Sorry is an easy word to say, Mr. Jackson. It doesn't change the situation." Tyler flinched at the hard tone and Lydia found her anger dissipating. Tyler Jackson wasn't Steven Winters. "But thank you anyway," she added in a softer voice.

By the end of the day Lydia was more tired from her numerous visitors than from the series of X-rays. The hardest person she had had to deal with hadn't been Tyler Jackson, but Anthony. Again he had broached the subject of her working with the company as a choreographer and teacher. Anthony had always been a demanding person to work for, so it hadn't surprised her that he wanted an answer when she had none.

Lydia massaged her temples, a dull headache intensifying as she recalled their conversation. More than ever she realized she needed to get away from New York or Anthony would be at her apartment every afternoon, trying to convince her she had something to offer the company. She wasn't so sure, though, and she certainly wasn't in any condition to make a major decision about her future until she could at least walk again. She felt as though she were floating in air, suspended, motionless.

For someone who had always known exactly what she wanted to do with her life, she hated this feeling of uselessness.

Jason was right. Hawaii was the answer. If there had been any doubt before about going there, after seeing Anthony and two fellow dancers in the company earlier, all doubt had been removed. In a few weeks she would be in Hawaii and for the first time she felt as if she might be able to cope with the months of therapy that lay ahead.

Steven sat in the audience watching Lydia dance across the stage. Her face was beautiful, full of poignant expression as the music built to its climactic finish. Her arms floated through the air, a graceful extension of her slim body. Steven's gaze traveled downward and widened in horror at the sight of the wheelchair. His attention swerved back to her face and her dark look accused him.

Steven bolted upright in bed and slowly oriented himself to his surroundings. He was in his bedroom at his New York apartment. He quaked with relief, running a shaky hand through his sleep-tousled hair.

He had returned to New York late the previous night and had fallen into bed, partly from exhaustion after his business trip to Europe but mostly from his lack of sleep over the last month.

Reaching for a pack of cigarettes on his nightstand, he grabbed one, lit it, and inhaled deeply. Relaxing back against the headboard, he exhaled, watching the curl of smoke spiral upward. Ever since Tyler had called him two weeks before to tell him that Lydia Masters had found out about his paying her hospital

bills anyway and had refused the money again, the
same dream had tormented him. He was in the first ring
at the New York State Theater watching a ballet with
her dancing the female lead. It would start out with her
on point, but by the end of the performance in the last
pas de deux she would be in a wheelchair. He was
beginning to hate the mere thought of climbing into
bed.

Steven laughed bitterly. He was a man known for his
relentless determination and ruthless decisions, and yet
he couldn't get Lydia Masters to accept conscience
money. He didn't blame himself completely for her
accident, but he felt he was partially at fault for not
totally concentrating on his driving that day; business,
as usual, had occupied his thoughts to the exclusion of
everything else.

Swinging his legs off the bed, he stabbed his cigarette
out in an ashtray, then rose, slipping on his velour robe
and belting it. He strode to the large window that
afforded him a view of the East River. Opening the
draperies, he stared at the pink and gray dawn.

He had been running from Lydia for more than a
month, using the excuse of his meetings in Europe as
the reason he had fled New York. In truth, something
had twisted deep into his heart when he had looked into
her face at her delicate porcelain features, like those of
a china doll. Then later when he had heard who she
was, the knife had cut even deeper. All of New York
had praised her brilliant talent and graceful beauty.

He had always admired someone with unique talent,
because he had once wanted to pursue a career as a
classical guitarist. Now it had been years since he had

even touched a guitar. After his father's death he had
had to fight tooth and nail to save Wintercom from
bankruptcy, and slowly, working for the company had
become a way of life for him. He had had a lot of
foolish dreams at the age of twenty-one, all of them
pushed aside for the company and his family.

Steven turned away from the window and headed for
the bathroom to shower. He needed to be at work
early. There would be a lot to do in the next few weeks
because he had been absent for over a month.

Sometime today I have to see Lydia Masters, he
thought as he stepped under the cool water. He had to
make time in his busy schedule to go up to the hospital
to see her. He would persuade her to take the money.
Then once and for all he would be free of this guilt.

After dressing in a three-piece gray suit, Steven
grabbed a cup of coffee and left his apartment to hail a
cab. He was examining some contracts in the backseat
of the taxi when his movements halted in midair. He
usually drove to work, but without thinking he had
taken a cab. Exasperated at himself, he tried to concentrate on the papers, but the feeling of having no control
over his life stayed with him. He didn't even want to
drive his Lotus anymore.

It wasn't until one-thirty that Tyler entered Steven's
office to give him a report on the Fielding acquisition.
Tyler sat opposite him at the conference table going
over the points in the deal, but halfway through he
stopped, studying Steven intently.

"Have you heard one word I've said?" Tyler asked.

"Yes. Yes," Steven said impatiently, waving his hand
in the air. "I trust your judgment, Tyler."

Tyler appeared surprised, but said nothing for a long moment. "Okay, Steven, out with it. What's on your mind? Last month you were telling me I was handing a sweet deal to Fielding on a silver platter."

"Well, are you?" Steven looked at him purposefully.

"No. The deal is a fair one for both parties involved, as you wanted."

"Then leave the papers and I'll go over them later. I want to go to the hospital to see Lydia Masters. I'll have just enough time before my three-thirty appointment."

"She's not there. I found out this morning that she checked out of the hospital a few days ago."

"Then I'll see her at her apartment. You have the address, don't you?"

"Yes, but she's gone. She left New York yesterday morning for Hawaii."

"Why in the hell did she do that?" He needed to see her. Didn't she understand that?

Tyler placed his notepad in his briefcase, then snapped it close. "I don't have an answer to that question, Steven. The few times I saw her she wasn't exactly confiding in me." He stood, staring down at Steven. "But something is eating away at you, friend. You're not your usual self since the accident."

Steven rose and faced Tyler across the table, leaning into it with his hands braced on top. "Do you know what it feels like to have hit a human being? To be responsible for pain, for the fact I've deprived her of her dancing? There have probably been times Lydia Masters wished I had killed her that day with my car. Her whole existence was her dancing."

"But damn it, Steven, she ran out into the street from between parked cars. You're not superhuman."

"I wish I were. Then I could walk away from this situation and not blame myself. Or maybe the accident might never have occurred if I had been."

"You haven't taken a vacation in years, Steven. Take one now. When you come back, you'll think differently about all of this. Everyone has his limits and I think you've reached yours. Work can't be your whole life."

"I can't. I've been gone for more than a month, Tyler. Longer than I had planned, because of the trouble in Paris." The tension in Steven's body drained away as though he were defeated.

"Yes, you can. Eric has been doing all right in your absence. I'll continue to keep a close eye on him and there's always the telephone." Tyler grinned wryly.

Steven turned away and walked toward his desk. "I don't know. I'll think about it."

Tyler crossed the room, mounting frustration apparent in his strides. "You are Wintercom, but the company won't fall apart without you for a few weeks."

Steven sat back in his chair, forming a steeple with his hands. "Where would you suggest I go?"

"Anywhere. The Bahamas or Mexico," Tyler answered in a tight voice. "Just get away and relax."

"How about Hawaii?"

"You won't let this go, will you?"

Steven smiled, a smile full of self-mockery. "Remember, I'm supposed to be relentless and determined."

"I'd say stubborn is a better word."

"I have to see her, Tyler. I ran when I should have

stayed. I've never done that before. Until I've settled my score with Lydia Masters, I'm not a free man."

Steven sat in the den of his mother's house waiting for her to come downstairs. He reached for a recent news magazine and was absently flipping through it when he suddenly stopped. A cold chill swept through him as he stared at the photograph of Lydia Masters at the Honolulu airport in a wheelchair. He couldn't take his eyes off the delicate features that were thinner than he remembered. The expression on her face tore him in two. It was obvious she hadn't been pleased about having her picture taken in a wheelchair.

Steven threw the magazine down and surged to his feet. He felt like a caged tiger. Restless, he paced the den, wishing his mother would hurry. His gaze was drawn back to the magazine and again he imagined the almost gaunt features of Lydia Masters. He swore and looked away.

"Steven, honey, it's good to see you. I'm glad you called this afternoon."

He whirled around at the sound of his mother's voice.

Vera Winters walked into the den. "Do you mind if Eric joins us for dinner? He called today a few minutes after you did."

"Mother, you never give up where we're concerned. This is your belated birthday dinner, so if you want Eric there, then it's fine with me." Steven dropped into a chair across from the couch and deliberately avoided looking at the magazine lying on the coffee table in front of him. "I'm sorry, it took me a couple of days to clear off my desk enough to arrange this dinner."

Vera, seated on the couch, smiled. "Son, I accepted your ways a long time ago. In fact, I feel I'm the main reason you're at Wintercom fifteen hours a day." She examined Steven sharply. "What's wrong? Are you having trouble with Wintercom? I told you seventeen years ago and I'll tell you now that this house is important to me but not at the expense of you or Eric. If you need money, I can sell—"

"Mother, why would you think the company was in trouble?"

"There's a look in your eyes that I've never seen before. You're usually so closed, but this is different. I can sense it. Wintercom means so much to you that I just naturally assumed that if something was wrong that it had to do with the company."

Steven shook his head, forcing himself to grin. "Mother, I'm fine. Just tired from the trip. I've decided to take a few weeks off and take a vacation. I'm leaving at the end of the week for Hawaii."

Vera sighed, relaxing back on the couch. "Great! It's about time, Steven. Are you leaving Eric in charge?"

"No, he isn't," Eric answered from the doorway. He pushed himself away from the doorjamb and entered the den. "As usual, brother dear has left a few watchdogs to keep me at bay."

Steven didn't want to fight with his brother that evening, so he ignored the comments. "I made a reservation for dinner at the inn. If we're going to make it, we should be leaving in a few minutes."

Eric sat down next to his mother on the couch and leaned back, his legs crossed casually. On the surface he seemed very relaxed, but Steven saw the antagonism in his brother's eyes. For the past three days Steven had pushed himself to catch up on his work enough to leave in two days, and if something wasn't said now to Eric, the dinner would be one long war.

"Before we go, Eric, I want to get one thing straight. I won't discuss Wintercom this evening. This is Mother's night and if you want to join us, you'll have to respect that."

"I only stopped by to tell Mother I'm not going to come after all. I wouldn't want to spoil one of the few evenings you do spend with Mother, so I made other plans. Don't worry about me, I'll have a great time on my own."

"I'm sure you will," Steven said.

"Steven! Eric! Stop it. You two are brothers."

"You don't have to remind me, Mother. I've never been able to forget that Steven's my big brother who can do *everything*." Eric strode toward the door. "Have fun on your vacation, Steven. I'll take real good care of the company. I wouldn't want anything to happen to my meal ticket."

Steven's hands clamped the arms of the chair while the expression on his face remained bland. "Well, then, I'm glad the company is going to be in such good hands," he drawled sarcastically.

Eric saluted Steven. "Good night, brother. Mother, I'll call you later."

"The undercurrents between you two seem to have gotten worse lately," Vera said after Eric had gone.

Steven released his tight grip on the chair. "I'm not sure why, but in the last six months Eric has been openly hostile at work."

"Have you given him any more responsibilities?"

"No, I've been so busy that I haven't had time to acquaint him with other aspects of the business."

"Maybe it's time you did."

Steven glanced at his watch. "Let's not talk about business tonight. We'd better leave if we're going to be on time for our reservation."

As they were leaving, Vera placed a hand on her son's arm. "Please consider what I said about Eric when you get back from Hawaii."

"I will, Mother." Steven hoped by then he would be free to turn his complete attention to the problem; after tonight he realized he couldn't continue to ignore Eric's resentment.

Chapter Four

Steven leaned against the redwood railing, breathing deeply of the flower-scented air. The pounding of the surf and the occasional call of a bird were the only sounds in the quiet of dawn. The sky was a brilliant mauve along the horizon, with the pale blue of a cloudless day overhead. It would be an exquisite, perfect day—a direct contradiction to his mood.

Having arrived late the night before, Steven hadn't seen the lush greenery surrounding his rented house until now. It only heightened the feeling that he was a loner. His work and position had isolated him from humanity, even his family and Tyler.

After he had pulled a few strings and paid an enormous price, he had been able to rent this house on Kauai next to Lydia's brother's. Now that he was close to her, he suddenly didn't know how he was going to meet her. Maybe I should just walk up to her and say, "Hi, I'm Steven Winters, the man who ran you down."

"I bet she would just love that," Steven muttered, craning his neck to get a glimpse through the trees of the house next door.

Steven realized he hadn't planned his moves at all, which was definitely unusual for him. He had gotten on the plane in New York with no idea how or what he was going to say to Lydia Masters. Always before, he had carefully thought through his strategy when confronting a difficult situation. *But then I've never had a problem like this one,* he thought with a twist of irony.

Something moving caught his attention. Through the lush tropical bushes and trees that formed a natural barrier around Lydia's place, Steven saw her making her way in the wheelchair along a path of wooden planks that led toward the beach. She stopped just short of the sandy area and stared at the ocean. For a long time she didn't move but sat very still watching the sun rise.

Lydia stared at the big waves that crested and broke onto the beach, but she was so lost in her own private world that she really didn't see them with any appreciation for their forceful beauty. She had lived in her wheelchair for a week and felt like a prisoner awaiting the death sentence. She kept telling herself that she only had to be in it for about four more weeks, but that seemed a lifetime away.

Finally the sound of the surf pulled her out of her thoughts and she blinked, realizing that the sun was up and that she needed to get back indoors before the tourists began to populate the beach. Her brother's house was in an isolated area of Kauai, but during the course of the day people who lived around there flocked to the beach to enjoy the beauty of a warm paradise.

With a frown Lydia scanned her surroundings. Ferns and flowering bushes were everywhere. *This place is heaven . . . and it is hell,* she thought, her eyes flicking to the metal contraption beneath her.

She maneuvered the wheelchair around with some difficulty, because she could only use one arm, and headed back up the path that led to her brother's house. For the past few days she had come outside only at sunrise. After that scene at the airport in Honolulu, she couldn't handle a possible crowd or confrontation. She had arrived at the same airport only a year before while on tour. Just as before, there had been a crowd of well-meaning fans who had greeted her, but this time she had hardly heard what they said. The looks of pity on their faces were stamped in her mind forever. It had taken her two days to get over their welcome, closeted in her brother's house speaking to no one who called, especially the reporters. Finally on the third day she did talk with her brother to thank him for equipping the house and grounds for a wheelchair.

Katie McPherson, her physical therapist, was waiting for her when she returned to the terrace. Katie had flaming red hair, sparkling blue eyes, and a ready smile. At first Lydia had had a hard time responding to the congeniality of her therapist, but Katie's good nature was difficult to ignore for long.

"I have the coffee on. What would you like for breakfast?"

"Just a piece of toast."

"Are you sure you won't join me for eggs and bacon?"

Lydia looked up, laughing softly. "You don't give up, do you, Katie McPherson?"

"Well, you are a wee bit of nothing."

"Okay, I'll try one egg. I've never eaten much of a breakfast until I came here."

"Breakfast is the best meal of the day. The most important one."

Katie left Lydia outside on the terrace. Lydia decided to soak up some sunshine for a few more minutes and relaxed back in the wheelchair. An early morning crispness still lingered in the air. The towering mountains were in stark contrast to the sandy beaches.

Finally Lydia wheeled herself into the house and toward the dining room where she and Katie always ate. Her wheelchair wouldn't fit through the kitchen door, so she was confined to certain parts of the house.

Katie placed a plate before Lydia with one egg, a piece of toast, and two strips of bacon. "You're certainly stubborn," Lydia said, looking up with a grin on her face.

"I have to be. I won't let my patients give up, and that requires a cool will and a stubborn streak," Katie replied as she sat down. "I'll clean up the dishes, then we'll have our therapy session."

They ate their meal in silence, Lydia concentrating on the task of eating and avoiding thoughts of the strenuous session that would follow. She knew she would walk again, but she also knew from her sessions already with Katie and at the hospital that it would be a long, frustrating path; the impulse to stand up and just walk was very strong.

After breakfast, Katie cleared away the dishes and Lydia moved to the piano in the living room. She loved to play. Before it had been the one pastime she had permitted herself other than listening to music. There had been no other time in her life for anything else except her dancing.

She fingered the ivory keys, playing a scale. Now she had a lot of time on her hands and didn't know how to fill it. Lydia played a piece, using only her one hand, but halted halfway through it when she realized it was from a ballet she had danced many times.

She slammed the cover down over the piano keys. She couldn't even do the one thing she loved besides dancing without being inundated with memories. She stared at the large picture window that afforded her a majestic view of the beach and ocean and in her mind she imagined the iron bars that trapped her in the house.

"Are you ready, Lydia?" Katie asked as she entered the living room from the kitchen.

Nodding, Lydia looked away from the picture window, making an effort to hide her feelings. The quiet seclusion of her surroundings was the balm she needed, but at times she felt as though she had been sentenced to solitary confinement. Maybe she had been wrong to turn away from her family and friends and rely completely on herself. She wasn't the same person she was before the accident. It was hard to handle the stranger within herself.

Katie grasped Lydia's free arm at the wrist and right

above her elbow. With her arm across her front, Lydia pushed up and out into Katie's hands.

"Hold. Hold," Katie said, offering resistance to Lydia. "Hold. Relax." Katie smiled. "You're in good shape. That will help when you learn to use crutches."

They ran through manual resistance with both arms and then the legs. All her life Lydia had been used to physical exertion, but as with everything else in her life, now even that was different, too. It didn't take much to exhaust her, and she was aggravated with her limited energy.

The next morning at dawn Lydia was at her usual spot under the ironwoods overlooking the beach, staring at the ocean without really seeing it. Her mind was filled with her conversation with Anthony the day before. Why did he have to call her? She had left New York to be completely away from the dance world and with one short conversation she was immersed in it again.

Anthony meant well, but his constant entreaty was taking its toll on her emotionally. Finally in anger and frustration she had told him not to call her again, that she would call him when she was ready, if she ever was ready.

A movement out of the corner of her eye riveted her attention to the man jogging by her, not fifteen feet away. Panicked, she placed her hand on the rail to turn the wheelchair around and flee before he caught sight of her. But it was too late. The stranger, not slowing a step, looked her directly in the eye and nodded, then returned his attention to the beach in front of him.

Slowly the panicky feeling subsided and other sensations took over, the most intense one—a feminine interest. In that brief moment when his keen gray eyes had locked with hers, her heartbeat had increased, her eyes had widened. His gaze had electrified her senses as though his eyes had courted hers across the sand.

Watching his retreating figure, she was disconcerted. A myriad of sudden impressions darted through her mind. His tall, beautifully proportioned body, his sinewy hardness, his legs that were columns of male power, his movements that were smooth and fluid as a dancer's all exuded a forceful grace. Lydia found herself admiring the athletic prowess in the stranger until he disappeared from her view.

She wanted to push the wheelchair out of her way and stand to join him. Frustration constricted her stomach muscles, and she was impaled with the familiar tormenting desire to feel the freedom of movement again.

A frown lined her face as she made her way laboriously back to the house where Katie waited on the terrace for her as usual. They had established a routine and suddenly Lydia hated the predictability of it all. She had always had a routine: morning classes, rehearsals, then performances in the evening. But the rest of her life had been impulsive, full of spontaneity. She wished she had that unconstrained feeling back, but how could she be spontaneous when she could hardly move?

Lydia greeted Katie with a nod, then proceeded inside the house to begin her day. It dragged by, as every day before it had, except for a few moments in the middle of the afternoon when Lydia sat by the picture window gazing down at the beach. The stranger was sunbathing, and she had a strong impulse to wheel herself outside at least onto the terrace to observe him better.

She thought about it and quickly dismissed the urge. However, she stayed by the window, watching, a picture of him jogging by her that morning as clear as if he were in the room with her. She could recall his muscles rippling as he jogged, the whipcord strength of his body moving as one finely tuned unit, and she was appalled at her fantasies.

Maybe she should have gone shopping with Katie. No, the stares of passersby were unnerving. Until she could walk out the front door, she wouldn't leave the house except to go to the hospital for X-rays.

After a restless night with her casts bothering her more than usual, Lydia awakened early and struggled to dress. Like the waves continuously pulled toward the shore, the beach drew her that morning more than any other day during the past week.

Outside, the salty breath of the ocean breeze whipped her long dark brown hair about her face. The muted colors of dawn painted the horizon as she brought her wheelchair to a halt.

She had taken a book with her this morning because she hadn't wanted the stranger to think she had been waiting for him to come by. It was a ridiculous thought, she acknowledged with a silent laugh. After all, she was here first. But as she tried to read she couldn't concentrate on the printed page.

A feeling of being watched caused her to raise her gaze, centering it on the man jogging toward her.

Casually he shifted his incredible eyes to fasten on hers. His were the color of the ocean during a storm, steel gray frothed with whitecaps.

Slowly his neutral expression altered, a smile slashing across his lean, dark face as he said "Hello" in a voice warm and husky.

Then he was jogging past her.

His brief, intent regard of her produced a tight aching dryness in her throat, and she swallowed several times, but nothing relieved the parched sensation.

That day sped by faster for Lydia because she couldn't wait to go to bed so that the next morning would come quicker. Again he was out on the beach sunning in the afternoon but so were other people. Lydia contented herself with observing him from the picture window, just as she had the day before. She was intrigued with "her stranger." Feelings that she had thought were buried surfaced as her eyes followed his progress to the water where he cooled off from the relentless sun.

At dawn the next day, Lydia was positioned under the grove of ironwoods, willowy pines with long, thin needles that swayed in the slightest breeze. She wondered why in the world she was carrying on so, just looking for trouble and setting herself up to be hurt. Though she tried to convince herself of this, still she stayed. For the first time since the accident, her interest was aroused and she couldn't let her new found hobby go.

She was afraid to look, though, down the beach in the direction he always came, so she kept her eyes diverted, trained on the rolling waves that continuously hammered at the beach. Her stomach churned with mixed feelings like the water stirring the sand. Several times she started to leave, then stopped and instead waited.

As the morning before, she felt his presence before she saw him. This time, though, instead of him jogging past her, a few long strides placed him in front of her where he paused.

"Hello again. You must enjoy the early morning hours as much as I do."

His voice was low and deep, an almost intimate quality to it that was disarming. A paralysis seized Lydia's throat, preventing her from replying. Silvery sparks of humor glittered in his eyes as a smile crinkled the corners.

Lydia's poise, developed from years of performing before huge audiences, was restored. "It's always so quiet and peaceful at this time of day."

His gaze, deep and intense, studied her closely as she had secretly evaluated him from the picture window. Her inner tension was betrayed by her grip on the arm of her wheelchair, and she withdrew behind a cool mask, mentally preparing herself for the usual look of pity that came with people's observations.

But there was none as his eyes slowly reestablished contact with hers. Instead, there was a frankly appreciative regard in them and Lydia wasn't prepared for that.

"Yes, quite different from New York City."

Lydia was staring at the dimples caused by his smile when he spoke. "New York?" Her gaze flew to his eyes. "You live in the city?"

He nodded. "I'm here on vacation. Are you vacationing, too? Or do you live here?"

They were simple, logical questions, but suddenly Lydia didn't want to answer, to give any of her self away. A closed expression entered her eyes. "Neither." The answer was abrupt, ending their conversation.

The stranger's smile faltered for a few seconds, then his dimples reappeared as he said, "Good day."

Lydia alternated between anger at herself for scaring him off and relief that he was gone. She chastised herself for acting foolishly. Either she wanted to talk to the man, or she didn't want to.

The following morning Lydia was at her place, determinedly staring straight ahead. The fighting spirit in her made her get up and dress. During the past weeks she had retreated so much from the outside world that she wouldn't give up this special time on the beach.

Lydia stayed until the sun was high in the sky, but he didn't appear! A few people had even come out to sunbathe, and still Lydia didn't move. Finally when she had received a few curious stares from the sunbathers down the beach, she headed back toward the house, strangely disappointed.

It was her own fault, she berated herself as she went up the ramp to the redwood deck. *Why would he show any interest after yesterday? He probably only stopped to be polite and with your rudeness he doesn't even feel that now.*

Later that morning during her therapy session with Katie nothing seemed to go right. Her temples pounded like the surf against the beach during a storm.

She was exhausted with the exercises before she had run through half of them. Pleading a headache, Lydia quit and retreated to lie in her darkened bedroom, her arm covering her forehead, her eyes closed.

The distant sound of the ocean soothed her and she relaxed. She listened to the chirping of a cardinal outside her window and wondered if he was calling his mate. She envied the bird its freedom and its mate; she had neither and wished she had both.

In her mind, her life—past, present, and future—stretched before her like a tightly woven tapestry. Slowly she watched as the fibers unraveled until there was nothing left. Her eyes bolted open and she struggled to a sitting position, orientating herself to the bedroom. For the first time she allowed free reign to the frightened feeling that she had suppressed since Jason had told her she couldn't dance again. A cold sweat broke out on her forehead; her hands trembled. She had a past and a present, but there was no future; the realization struck terror in her.

A soft knock at the door coupled with Lydia's innate resilience pushed the overwhelming fear to the back of her mind. "Yes."

Katie poked her head through the doorway. "Your brother is on the phone. Do you want me to bring the phone in here?"

"Yes, please."

Lydia was glad Jason was calling. It would take her mind completely away from her troubling thoughts. Katie plugged the phone in, then quietly left the room as Lydia picked up the receiver.

"Hi, Sis," Jason said in a cheerful tone. "Before I go

down for rehearsal, I wanted to check and see how things were going with my favorite sister."

"Your only sister," she corrected with a laugh. "And things are okay."

"That's good, because when I see you next I want you to walk into my arms."

"I'd have it no other way. How's Maggie doing?"

There was a lengthy silence on the other end of the line, and Lydia knew before her brother said anything that the news wasn't good.

"No change. I put the house on the market, though. Maggie's therapist seems to think it's a good idea for both of us to start fresh somewhere else."

"How long will you be at Lake Tahoe?"

"Just another week. I'm thinking of retiring completely from performing. I love to sing but this life is hard on me and especially hard on Maggie. Do you realize, Lydia, that I hardly know her? I've been gone so much that when I was at home I was a stranger to my own daughter. I have a lot to make up for."

"Then Hawaii will be a new start for you, too."

"In a way, yes. See you in about a month."

When Lydia placed the receiver back in its cradle, the word "stranger" played over and over in her mind, instantly bringing her thoughts back to the man on the beach. Suddenly she wanted another chance to speak with him, to get to know him.

Steven sat, leaning back, at the paper-cluttered dining room table that serviced as a makeshift desk, his elbows resting on the arms of the chair with his fingers laced together. He didn't like the way things were going with his Paris deal but especially with Lydia Masters. Deep in thought, he didn't realize the phone was ringing until finally the blaring shrill pierced his mind with its persistence.

Bolting forward, he reached for the phone and growled into the mouthpiece, "Winters speaking."

"Steven, we have a problem. Fielding has decided not to sell after all," Tyler said.

A tightness in Steven's expression was the only evidence of his anger. "It's just a ploy to have us come begging. Find another company that will suit our purposes. I won't pay any more for it than I've already offered."

"I would like to have one more talk with Fielding before we shop around. He's been out of touch with his company and I think it's a few top men at Fielding Corporation talking to him that changed his mind. They're scared of their jobs if we take over."

"And they're damn right to be scared. I won't have incompetents working for Wintercom." Slowly the tautness drained from his expression, and Steven relaxed again, leaning back in the chair. "Do what you think is necessary. By the way, did you ask Eric's advice?"

"No."

"I want you to. He needs the experience."

There was a long pause.

"Steven, Eric hasn't been into the office since you left for Hawaii."

The old adage, while the cat's away the mouse will play, popped into Steven's thoughts. He gritted his teeth, fighting the mounting disappointment.

"Where is he?"

"I'm not sure. I think Bermuda for a long weekend that turned into a vacation."

"Use any means you have to, but I want my brother back in New York and at least showing up every day at Wintercom. If he argues, tell him I will conveniently forget to pay his check for the next month. That ought to do it."

"Okay. But I don't know what good it's going to do. When are you returning to New York?"

Steven hesitated, recalling the previous day when Lydia had withdrawn so quickly behind a cool front. *It won't be easy to get to her.* "I'm not sure, Tyler. Maybe next week. Is everything going all right? Have you heard from Paris yet?"

"No, not yet. Except for that problem with Fielding, everything's fine. If anything important comes up, I'll call. Take some time off and enjoy. Wintercom will be in one piece whenever you decide to come back. You left a very efficient organization."

Steven smiled, a thin smile that tightened his lips. "Thanks, Tyler."

After hanging up, he rose and walked to the window. He could almost see the surprised look on Tyler's face as he had said, "Thanks, Tyler." It wasn't that he didn't appreciate the people at Wintercom who did a good job. It was just that he rarely said thank you. He wasn't sure why he had to Tyler moments before, except that he did appreciate the work Tyler did for the corporation.

Steven's gaze strayed to the spot where Lydia usually sat in the morning. Of course it was empty. He had wanted to be back out on the beach at dawn this morning, but he had overslept, something he never did. He had to wonder at all the things he was doing lately that departed from his usual routine.

Looking back on the morning, he shook his head in puzzlement. He had shot out of bed and out the door so quickly that he had only been wearing his pajama bottoms. From the redwood deck, though, he had seen that Lydia had left the beach, and with disappointment he had made his way back into the house to dress properly. He hadn't gone out to sun himself as he had the days before, but instead had worked through the morning and afternoon as if he were in New York.

Steven walked to the bar and fixed himself a stiff drink. It was dinnertime and he didn't look forward to eating alone; he wanted to barge over to the house next door and demand that Lydia have dinner with him.

Outside on the deck he lowered himself into a lounge chair and sipped his drink. Lydia Masters was a beautiful woman and he was finding it more difficult to get her out of his mind. He had overslept that morning after having spent a restless night with the recurring nightmare.

With a resolution firmly in his mind to speak with her the next day, Steven finished his drink, prepared himself a sandwich, then wrapped up a few business details before heading to bed early. He had no intention of oversleeping again.

The following morning the shrill sound of the alarm jolted Steven awake. He fumbled to turn it off, then swung his legs to the floor and stood. Glancing at the window, he saw the gray predawn sky and quickly dressed in a T-shirt and shorts.

When Steven stepped out onto the redwood deck, he

noticed Lydia under the largest ironwood by the beach, staring at the waves tumbling onto the shore. To him the tall pine tree, towering above the others, stood alone and straight, mirroring the proud independence that Lydia was striving to convey to the world. In that moment Steven felt the isolation that she had purposely created for herself. They stood like the two houses, secluded and private against outsiders. Suddenly Steven didn't want to be a stranger in Lydia's life and was determined to change that this morning.

Maybe "her stranger" had gone home, Lydia thought as she looked toward the gray dawn. It was going to rain and in her mind the darkness of the sky reflected her future.

She wasn't sure why she felt so disappointed that she might not see the stranger again. She had turned away from well-meaning friends and toward a man whose name was unknown to her. Maybe it was because she hadn't seen any pity in his eyes. Maybe it was because he had made her feel almost whole again when he had looked at her with those intense gray eyes. In his eyes she had seen a spark of interest, and she found she needed that male appreciation as she had never before needed it.

Since the sky was growing blacker, Lydia decided to go inside and was turning toward the house when she caught sight of him jogging down the beach. He stopped in front of her and grinned, a positively devilish grin.

"Hello, I'm glad the weather didn't keep you in today."

His greeting was spoken in velvet tones, like the lush

undergrowth around them. Her gaze drank in the welcome sight of him, noting the waves of coal black hair that feathered back from his face in disorder, the metallic gray of his eyes that was an effective shield against his inner thoughts, the tanned skin that was stretched over the commanding features. He had a manner and confidence that came naturally. His was a bold masculinity, almost primitive, much like the tropical mountains of the islands, untamed, wild. She felt abruptly trapped by his power; the feeling of being imprisoned was even more intense than when she had first sat in the wheelchair.

An eyebrow quirked upward. "I'm sorry if I disturbed you."

There was a hint of amusement in the statement that nullified the apology. She had been staring at him and the laughing delight in his eyes told her that he didn't mind. In fact, he matched her intent evaluation with one of his own. Her flustered discomfort quickly evolved into embarrassment that just as quickly became elation at the glint of male interest in his eyes.

"You didn't." Her voice was a breathless quaver. She couldn't withstand the warmth in his regard. It took a great deal of effort to continue in a much stronger voice, "Do you jog every morning?" *And why didn't you come by yesterday?*

"Whenever I can."

The stranger sat on a fallen log a few feet away, his hands dangling between his legs. He was a picture of complete relaxation while inside she was a mass of nerves, pulled tight and ready to snap at any moment.

"Which isn't as often as I wish," he added a few seconds later.

There was an element of mystery to this meeting that sharpened her feminine awareness. She knew nothing about him except that he lived in New York City, and yet she had allowed him into her life. That realization came to her paired with another the same instant. She wanted to get to know him much better.

"My name is Lydia."

She didn't offer her last name because she didn't want to take the chance that he might know of her and look down with that pitying look she had grown to loathe. Of all the people, she suddenly realized that she couldn't take it from this man before her. She sensed she wouldn't be able to turn away from him with her head held high if he did.

He hesitated for a moment, his eyes drilling into her as though he were trying to read her secret thoughts. He cleared his throat, then said, "I'm Steve."

Chapter Five

*S*teve! For an instant, an angry spark flickered in Lydia's eyes. Then just as quickly, it vanished. *Steve is not Steven.* A smile recaptured her features.

"I'm glad you stopped this morning—Steve."

Steve glanced toward the sky then back at Lydia. "I don't think it would be such a good idea to be caught too far away from the house. At any moment it looks like the bottom will fall out of the sky. And frankly, talking with a beautiful woman has always held more appeal for me than jogging in a rainstorm."

Lydia shifted slightly in her chair at the compliment, her eyes fixed on the tips of his running shoes. "To tell you the truth, jogging has held no appeal to me."

"I had to find a way to combine the time I needed to be alone with something to keep me in shape. Jogging fit the bill. I usually jog in Central Park when I can find the time."

"Alone?" Lydia laughed, the sound warm and rich like the heavy, moisture-laden air. "In Central Park?"

His laughter rumbled from deep within his chest. "I know there are hordes of people around, but when I jog I do feel alone. Have you ever done something that makes you feel that way?"

"Yes" was her quiet reply. *My dancing,* she thought.

"Well, then, you know what I mean. In New York a person has to find ways to be alone, which isn't easy. Now, here in Hawaii there's no problem. Here there are places that seem so untouched. You certainly can't find that in New York City."

"The amount of people around has nothing to do with loneliness or isolation."

He rubbed his jaw, a dark shadow of a day's growth of beard on it. "Are you a loner?"

"In a sense, yes."

His eyes lowered to the wheelchair. "Because of that?"

Lydia inhaled a deep breath. The conversation was getting too personal, she thought with a panic akin to what she had felt at her first audition.

"I'm sorry. I shouldn't have asked. I have no right." Steve stood, preparing to leave when the first drops of rain spattered his arm.

"I think the bottom is beginning to fall," Lydia said as she started to turn her wheelchair toward Jason's house.

Steve took the handgrips at the back of the wheelchair and began pushing Lydia toward the small ramp that gently sloped to the redwood deck. Lydia started to protest that she was capable of taking care of herself when the rain increased rapidly. Her protest died on her lips as the red T-shirt she wore quickly became plastered to her skin.

Before they reached the ramp, they were both soaking wet from the sudden downpour. Katie slid the glass door back, and Steve maneuvered the wheelchair quickly inside the house.

Lydia brushed her wet, stringy hair from her face. "I've only been up an hour and already I have to change clothes."

She gave into the desperate need to laugh; otherwise the feeling of inadequacy would overwhelm her. She had always been so independent that sitting in a wheelchair, unable to walk and dependent on other people for so much embarrassed her.

"Reminds me of when I was a kid," Steve replied, coming around to stand in front of Lydia. "Are you all right?"

The gentle question sobered Lydia and she smiled faintly. "I will be just as soon as I get into some dry clothes." She glanced back over her shoulder at the window then at Steve. "Katie's specialty is breakfast. Will you stay and eat with us?"

"I don't want to impose."

"Nonsense. There's no reason for you to go back out in the rain. You may use my brother's room to dry off in, and please borrow a pair of his shorts and one of his shirts."

While talking with him outside, Lydia had realized she enjoyed the company. She didn't want to be around people who had known her in the past, but she wasn't really a loner as she had implied. Only lately had she set herself apart from others. In the past she had always enjoyed company. Katie, and now Steve, were filling that need without the ties. She wanted to make a clean break from her other life; maybe that way she would survive the drastic change.

"Are you sure?" Steve asked, concern still apparent in his voice.

Lydia was suddenly aware of the rain striking against the windows. There were no lights on and the dark shadows played across Steve's strong features. A sudden tension filled the quiet room. She wasn't sure of many things anymore, but she was sure she wanted him to stay.

"I'll go on and begin getting breakfast," Katie said as she turned on a light, then started toward the kitchen.

Lydia stared into his gray eyes which absorbed everything and yet were so unfathomable. He seemed to block any hint of emotion, and Lydia was sure he must be a very private man.

"Yes, I'm sure, Steve. I'll show you to Jason's bedroom."

Lydia wheeled herself ahead of him, acutely conscious of his eyes on her. The back of her neck prickled, the sensation quickly spreading through her body. By the time she reached the door to Jason's bedroom, she felt dizzy from the feelings he was creating in her. Her passionate nature, which had always been expressed through her dancing, had lain dormant for too long.

When he passed her to enter the room, his hand brushed lightly across her arm, and she felt as if she had worked out too long and her whole body were quivering from the hard exercise. He turned back to her and smiled, and a silver light gleaming in his eyes further disrupted the normal functions of her body. As his gaze skimmed lower, taking in her clinging wet T-shirt, her blood ran rampant and her breathing grew more shallow.

Flashing him a smile, Lydia quickly moved away and didn't look back. Inside her bedroom she breathed easier, her heartbeat calming to a normal rate.

Tempering her thoughts concerning Steve, Lydia managed to dress without help and to return to the living room within fifteen minutes. Steve stood at the picture window watching the rain hammering at the ground, the beach and ocean barely visible through the downpour. His legs were braced apart, his hands clasped behind his back. His stance reminded her of the untamed fierceness of the ocean beyond the window during a storm.

Jason's shirt stretched enticingly across Steve's back. He was broader than Jason in the chest, but other than that her brother's clothes fit Steve well. She didn't speak. Instead, she admired his muscular build for the moment.

Slowly Steve turned to face her and the expression in his eyes altered. She wasn't sure but for a fleeting moment she thought she had seen a deep sadness there.

"Not a bad fit. I hung my wet clothes up to dry in the bathroom. Of course, from the looks of this storm it may not quit for a while." Steve crossed the room and sat in a chair near Lydia, so they were on eye level.

The thought of his not leaving for a few hours was as pleasant as the steady fall of the rain. "I hope this downpour didn't ruin any of your plans for the day," she said. "I would hate to go on a vacation and have it rain most of the time."

Steve leaned forward, resting his elbows on his thighs and clasping his hands together. A subtle tension laced the atmosphere, an anticipation, an eagerness springing up between them. "I had no specific plans." But his eyes said he wouldn't mind spending the time with her.

"Most people on vacation exhaust themselves being on the go the whole time. They feel they have to see everything," Lydia chatted nervously. His devastating look disarmed her.

He tipped back his head and laughed. "That's true, but I guess I haven't had much experience with vacations. This is my first one in years."

Lydia bent toward him as though to impart a deep dark secret. "In truth, this is my first in years, too."

"I can't believe I've found another workaholic."

"Breakfast is on the table," Katie announced from the dining room doorway.

Once Lydia had entered the dining room and positioned herself at the table, she said, "I'm sorry I forgot to introduce you two earlier. Katie McPherson, this is Steve . . ."

Steve extended his hand. "Wilson."

"I'm glad you could stay for breakfast, Mr. Wilson," Katie said as she sat down at the table.

"Steve, please. And it's nice not to have to fix something to eat for a change." He scanned the dishes on the table and added, "This is a feast. Do you always eat this much at breakfast?"

"Frankly, until Katie came along I hardly ate any breakfast at all. And now I think that one of her goals in life is to fatten me up."

"I like a hard task," Katie commented as she passed Steve the plate of pancakes, followed by the eggs and bacon.

"She has a point there. I think your body could stand a few banana splits and still be as slim as a reed."

Lydia tensed at his light teasing. She was slender because she had always had to watch her weight as a dancer; now there was no need to and she wished there was. She retreated from the conversation and was content with just listening to Steve tell Katie about New York City. Several times he tried to bring Lydia into the conversation, but she would answer in a one or two word sentence, then fall silent again.

After breakfast was over, Steve having taken care of any extra helpings left on the platters, Katie insisted on clearing away the dishes by herself.

When Katie was in the kitchen, Steve looked directly into Lydia's eyes and said, "Did I say something to upset you?"

The sincerity in his expression melted her reserve, and she shook her head.

The laugh lines at the sides of his eyes deepened, the dimples appearing in his cheeks. "I'm glad because I was hoping you'd play gin rummy with me."

"Gin rummy?" Both of Lydia's eyebrows rose.

"When I was a kid, I used to play cards on a rainy day to pass the time until I could go outside. I suddenly had the urge to do it again."

"Well, I'll have to admit you have picked one of the few card games I know. I think there are some cards in the table by the couch. If you'll get them, we can play in here at the dining room table."

Shortly Steve returned with two decks of cards and a pad and pencil. "What do you say to a penny a point?"

Through half-closed eyelids Lydia threw him a suspicious look. "Are you a card shark?"

"Me!" He acted offended, but there was a mocking glint in his eyes. "Whatever gave you that idea?"

"Oh, I don't know. Perhaps the way you casually brought up playing cards, then just as casually you mentioned playing for money." Although laughter tinged her words, her expression was serious.

"Okay. Then we won't play for money."

A suppressed smile diffused Lydia's serious expression. "That's okay. I'll take my chances."

Shaking his head, he said, "No. We'll change the stakes to something else."

"What?" Suddenly her every instinct was alert.

His gaze captured hers and he said in a voice sweet as honey, "If I win, you have to kiss me and if you win, I have to kiss you."

Lydia's eyes grew huge, the stakes titillating. "No, if I win, you have to tell me something about yourself. All through breakfast you talked around your life. A deal?"

"Sounds fair to me. But I have to warn you, Lydia, that I'm very lucky when it comes to cards."

He had said her name with such firm familiarity that Lydia was taken aback for a moment. Suddenly there was a sensual intimacy between them that prevailed throughout the game. The tension increased as Steven went on to lead a hundred points. Lydia was beginning to think that she was subconsciously throwing the game. Some of her discards had just been plain dumb.

"Gin rummy," he declared triumphantly, laying down his cards for her to see.

She placed her cards on the table and listened as he counted the points in her hand. She watched his large hand as he wrote his score down and added it to his other points. She wondered what his hands would feel like on her body; her skin was on fire from her vivid imagination. The picture of them entwined together made her blood run hot, regardless of the fact she didn't need any complications in her messed-up life.

"That's all I needed to win," he announced.

The triumphant gleam was gone. Instead, his eyes were sparked with a silver glint of desire. She was speechless, all her thoughts centered on his reward for winning the game. She wanted the kiss but at the same time was afraid of it.

In a trance, she watched him gather the cards into a neat stack. To her dazed mind, his actions seemed to be in slow motion, as if she were observing him from behind a two-way mirror. He avoided looking at her for a timeless moment.

Then when everything was picked up, Steve rose from his chair, his head twisting about, his eyes seeking hers. Their gazes embraced and became bound together with an urgent, sensual need. Towering above her, he slowly leaned over and cupped her chin in one hand to lift her face toward his. His hands settled on her shoulders as their lips touched softly, tentatively at first.

Her mouth moved against his, her lips parting to allow him free access to her honeyed cavern. His tongue plunged deep into the dark recesses and circled, exploring every minute crevice. The pressure of his hands on her shoulders increased as the kiss deepened to an ardent claim of victory. Whose victory Lydia wasn't sure, because in her mind she relished his savage possession as though she had been starving for weeks and was suddenly given food—a whole banquet.

When he straightened, neither spoke for a long moment. Lydia stared at the chair he had been sitting in, afraid to look up into his face. Suddenly she hated the wheelchair more than ever. It stood in her way like a thirty-foot wall.

Finally when she could no longer stand the silence, she glanced toward Steve, her teeth digging into her lower lip. He was looking out the window, his arms very straight at his sides, his back rigid. Lydia's heart sank, her teeth leaving indentations in her lip.

"The rain's finally stopped. I'd better change. I've intruded long enough today, Lydia."

Intruded? No, this was no intrusion.

But Lydia didn't say anything as Steve walked toward Jason's bedroom. Minutes passed and when he reentered, Lydia was still at a loss as to what to say to this man. She hardly knew him, but he had awakened feelings in her that had died the day of the accident.

In four strides he was across the room and at the sliding glass doors. Pausing, he looked back over his shoulder. "Thank you for the breakfast and the game of cards. I enjoyed the visit."

"You're welcome," Lydia managed to say, stunned at such extremely polite manners.

Steven held her glance for a few seconds longer, then slid the door open and left. Outside the refreshing, rain-drenched air cloaked him, but nothing cooled the fires in his veins. That kiss had ignited something deep inside that he hadn't known existed. He cared what happened to Lydia, not merely because he felt partially responsible for her accident, but because of the woman she was.

He had intended to tell her who he was, but for some

reason he hadn't been able to bring himself to say Steven Winters. One part of him had been appalled that he had lied, because he was known for his honesty. But the other part had been elated; he had seized a chance to get to know her and possibly help her through this difficult period. He knew she hadn't adjusted to her loss yet, was probably trying to ignore it; it was evident in her eyes, which were two mirrors of her soul and thoughts. No wonder she had been a great ballerina. She was so expressive that he doubted she could mask her true feelings from anyone for long.

When Tyler had told him Lydia wouldn't accept any financial assistance from him, he had felt helpless. He was a problem solver, always able to retain control of any situation he found himself in. That was so, until Lydia came along, he thought. Now, as Steve Wilson, he had a chance to gain control, to help her solve her problem.

As Steven entered his house, his steps were light and quick. He headed for the shower, whistling. With the cool water plummeting his back, Steven rationalized his intense reaction to the kiss. She was a beautiful woman; of course he would be attracted to her.

As he toweled himself dry he decided he would contact Tyler to inform him that he would be staying for another week. Steven picked up the phone in his bedroom and punched out the numbers of Wintercom.

"This morning I need to go into town and get some groceries." Dressed in her robe, Katie was heading for the kitchen to make a pot of coffee. "I could get an extra steak for dinner tonight if you'd like."

At the sliding glass doors Lydia glanced over her

shoulder at Katie, who had stopped and was wait-ing for an answer. Lydia was well aware of what Katie meant. Katie's one comment about Steve the day be-fore had been, "He's one hunk of a man." It hadn't gone unnoticed by Lydia that Katie had tactfully stayed away when they had been playing cards. *She probably thinks the best therapy is a good man*, Lydia decided, amusement in her green eyes. *And Katie might be right.*

"I may not see him again," Lydia said, hoping there was no truth in those words.

"Well, then one of us will eat the steak tomorrow night."

"Okay."

"Good. Now that that's settled, my brain needs some coffee. It's already been overtaxed without its early morning stimulant."

While Katie went into the kitchen, Lydia wheeled herself out to the edge of the beach, the sky aflame with a brilliant sunrise, reflecting her anticipation that she might see Steve again. As a new day dawned, Lydia relived her response to Steve's kiss. For a few minutes his male essence had possessed her with its seductive command. It had struck a chord within her very much like a sensuous ballet. For that short moment the only being that had mattered had been Steve Wilson, total-ly, absolutely.

There was an air of mystery about him, but she didn't care. In some ways it enhanced her attraction. It appealed to her impulsive side.

Lydia leaned forward slightly and looked up and down the beach, a frown slowly forming. The sun was high and there was no sign of Steve. Her doubts continued as fifteen minutes passed and still no Steve.

She was a fool to have taken anything for granted. His kiss obviously had meant nothing to him except his prize for winning at gin rummy. She had isolated herself so much from the people who cared and loved her that she was reaching out to a perfect stranger to fill the void. And her hand had been slapped!

"Hello, Lydia. You look like you've been out for a while."

The rich timbre of Steve's voice was a welcomed reprieve. Lydia twisted about in the wheelchair and watched him stroll toward her, a picnic basket in his hand. She looked from Steve to the basket and said, "Hi." A smile radiated from her eyes. "I'm glad you came. Is that a new type of beach bag?"

He chuckled softly. "No. It's exactly what it appears to be. A picnic basket with food and all that good stuff. I hope you'll join me for breakfast."

"Here on the beach?"

"Yes, here on the beach. A picnic usually is outside. And today is certainly not like yesterday."

Lydia scanned the beach, conscious of a few people coming out to sunbathe. She hesitated.

"Lydia, the people who stare aren't worth your consideration," Steve said very quietly.

"But—"

"But, nothing. You're a beautiful woman, Lydia. Have you ever thought they may be staring because of that, not because you're sitting in a wheelchair?" He squatted down in front of her, taking one hand in his while he touched her face with his other. His hand lingered on her cheek in a silent worship of her beauty.

She tried to pull away. "You don't understand, Steve. I see what's in their eyes."

"I understand more than you think." His hold on her hand tightened, as if he were trying to impart some of his strength to her. "Do you want to tell me about it?"

Severing their visual contact, Lydia looked beyond Steve to the ocean: There was a light breeze, scented with flowers and the ocean, that cooled the warm air; there was a clear, cloudless sky; there were the melodies of nature, the birds, the sound of the surf, the rustling of the palm fronds. Suddenly Lydia didn't want to ruin the morning with memories.

She shook her head. "Not now, Steve."

"Will you stay and share this breakfast that I spent the last hour preparing?"

His hand fell away from her face, and suddenly Lydia wanted to grab his hand and place it back where it had been touching her. Her gaze drifted back to his proud, aggressive features, looking deeply into the silver-gray of his eyes. They held an appeal she couldn't resist.

"On one condition."

Steve rose. "What condition?"

"That you have dinner tonight at my house."

"That's a condition I can handle. What time?"

"Seven. You can cook the steaks."

He laughed as he opened the basket. "I see. First you invite me to dinner, then you make me cook."

"Didn't you know, Steve Wilson, that there's nothing free in life?"

Steve halted his movements in midair. "I know," he answered as a few seconds later he finished taking the Thermos of coffee out of the basket.

There was a subtle distancing between them, and

Lydia was puzzled as to the reason why. Then suddenly it came to her: There was something in Steve's life that he was running from or hadn't faced yet.

Steve snapped his fingers. "I forgot one important ingredient."

There was so much food, Lydia couldn't imagine what was missing. "I can't see what that could possibly be. You have fresh fruit, ham, cheese, toast, orange juice, and coffee. I don't even think I can eat half of that."

"The table and chair. Madame, this is a first class operation." He took off toward his house and reappeared with a card table and one folding chair a few minutes later.

When the table was set, Steve sat across from her and dished food onto his plate. "Lydia, I'm a man who pays his debts. Since I'm coming to dinner tonight at your place, I want to take you out to dinner tomorrow night to a little restaurant I discovered that has great—"

"No!" The refusal reverberated like the sound of the distant surf clashing against rocks.

He glanced up, his expression unreadable. "Why not?"

Lydia's mouth twisted into an ironic frown. "Isn't it obvious?"

Steve's eyes narrowed. "No. Maybe you should explain it to me."

"I'm in a wheelchair. I won't be seen out in public in this—thing. I won't!"

"Are you feeling sorry for yourself?"

The quiet question was like a physical blow, and Lydia instantly leaped to her defense. "You're damn right I am!"

"So you're going to deny yourself any pleasure and shut yourself up in that house?"

Tears crowded Lydia's eyes; she struggled to keep from crying. "It's enough I have to fight my own pity. I can't fight other people's, too. Steve, I've been in public and I've seen people look at me as though I have four legs."

The tensed line of his jaw and the compressed lips spoke of his rising anger. "The hell with those people! I told you they weren't worth your time," he growled, his slate-gray eyes boring into hers.

"It's not that simple." Her muscles seemed to liquefy; her body suddenly grew very weary. "In my work I've always drawn from people. I entertained. I can't just forget that."

"How long have you been in that wheelchair?"

Lydia stared at her plate, half filled with food, then slowly she lifted her eyes to meet the tender look in his. That was her undoing. She slumped back in her wheelchair, swallowing the lump in her throat. "Since leaving the hospital two weeks ago."

After admitting that, she told him about the accident, the operations, the prognosis and what she had done for a living before she had been hit by a car. When she was through, strangely she felt better having shared this with Steve. It was as if she finally had shut one door on her past and had taken a step forward toward coping with her future.

"Where do you want to go from here?"

He had a way of asking the most difficult questions, making her face the hard, cold facts of her situation. And for a moment she resented it.

"Is it that important? I'm not even walking yet!"

Lydia no longer heard the sounds of nature. She no longer saw the clear, cloudless sky nor the glittering silver blue of the ocean. She and Steve could have been anywhere for all she noticed as her eyes clashed with his.

"Yes, it's important, Lydia, and I think you know that."

Their gazes met across the expanse of the card table, hers filled with anger and resentment, his gently but insistently probing for answers she couldn't give.

Lydia broke the tethers that held them invisibly bound and picked up her fork. She moved the pieces of melon and pineapple around on her plate for a long moment before, exasperated, she let the fork slip from her fingers. She didn't have to look up to know that Steve was still staring at her.

"I don't know," she mumbled, then as she raised her head and tilted her chin at a proud angle, she said in a stronger voice, "I don't know what I want to do with the rest of my life. I feel lost with no purpose."

Steve sucked in a deep breath, his hand searching for hers and grasping it. "It's not easy starting over, but people have to do it all the time."

His soft-spoken words hurt. "Why are you being hard on me?"

His thumb began to rub back and forth across the palm of her hand, and she was distracted by the sensual touch. She couldn't take her eyes off their clasped hands.

"Do you want me to encourage you to wallow in self-pity or do you want me to encourage you to start looking for other ways to use your talent?"

She didn't answer his question. Steve didn't want an

answer, because her personality demanded only one response. Lydia was having a hard time thinking of anything to say as his thumb continued its tantalizing study of her hand then her wrist. Her whole arm felt as if it were on fire by the time Steve had completed his tactile inspection.

Steve compelled Lydia to look at him as he said, "Then I'll be patient and take things one step at a time. Will you have dinner with me tomorrow evening *at my house?* I'm a fair cook." As he threw in the last sentence, a grin slanted provocatively across his mouth. "I think," he added doubtfully.

Lydia closed her eyes for a moment, then opened them. "I would love to."

Chapter Six

𝒯he following day, with her head bent, Lydia slumped exhausted into her wheelchair after her therapy session, one arm hanging limply over the side, the other lying across her lap as if it weighed a ton.

"It won't be long, Lydia. The cast on the arm will be removed soon," Katie said.

"I want to walk tonight!" Lydia's head snapped up, her eyes hard, demanding. "I want to go to dinner at Steve's at least using crutches, not this damn thing." She waved her hand contemptuously at the wheelchair.

"You can't. It's that simple," Katie said angrily.

Lydia massaged the aching muscles of her neck, then rolled her head, wishing that she hadn't accepted his invitation for dinner the day before. *I can't go,* she thought frantically. *How am I going to get there*? *His house isn't equipped for a wheelchair.* She hadn't thought that far when she had told Steve she would come to dinner.

Lydia wheeled herself to the table where the phone was and picked up the receiver. She dialed the number he had given her the previous night, her muscles tensing as she waited for him to answer.

On the seventh ring when Lydia was about to hang up, Steve answered, "Hello."

"Steve, this is Lydia."

"This is a surprise. I was thinking seriously of letting the phone ring. I have reached a strategic and delicate maneuver in the dinner preparations."

His voice was a warm caress that made it difficult for Lydia to say why she was calling.

"Is something wrong, Lydia?"

A quick glance at her wheelchair fortified her resolve not to go to his house, and she replied, "I won't be able to come to dinner tonight, Steve." She forced her voice to remain cool, hoping to discourage any further discussion, but she felt hot as she pictured him lying on the beach earlier that day in his bathing suit. He was a man in superb physical condition while she sat, useless, in a wheelchair, unable to do the most ordinary, everyday chore.

Finally he broke the lengthy silence. "Why not, Lydia?"

His voice was a mixture of roughness and tenderness as though he knew exactly why she didn't want to come to dinner. Lydia closed her eyes and said, "I can't! Just leave it at that."

Her lids fluttering open, she stared straight into Katie's perplexed look, quickly replaced the receiver, then took the phone off the hook. Katie said nothing, though, as she turned away to straighten some magazines on the coffee table.

Lydia felt horrible. Everything in her life had changed in less than two months. She was like a newborn baby, having to relearn the simplest things in life.

"I'd better start dinner, then," Katie said, leaving for the kitchen.

Katie didn't have to voice her disappointment because Lydia could see it in her expression. Dinner the night before with Steve had been wonderful. He had entertained them until Lydia had forgotten her problems for a few short hours. She knew Katie thought Steve was good for her. He was! But still . . .

A loud pounding on the sliding glass door captured Lydia's attention. She looked up and saw Steve, a frown engraved on his handsome features. Katie quickly came into the living room, hurrying toward him.

Lydia wanted to shout, "Don't open that door," but she knew Steve wouldn't let a mere glass door stand in his way. The look on his face was one of adamant single-mindedness.

Lydia braced herself when he strode into the room and stopped a foot from her. "I suppose this is some more of your self-pity. You don't need other people to pity you. You do enough for everyone."

His voice was dangerously quiet, but the words battered at the wall she had erected between them. She squared her shoulders and lifted her chin, looking him straight in the eye. "I'm not pitying myself. I'm being practical, Steve Wilson. Neither one of us had thought of how I would get over to your house."

"Correction. You hadn't but I had. I'll carry you."

"No!" Her eyes widened at the suggestion.

"Why not? You hardly weigh anything and even with your casts on your leg and arm, I think I can manage. I'm in reasonably good condition."

Without thinking, Lydia let her gaze travel the length of him, dressed in navy blue shorts and a white knit shirt.

"Surely you can see that," Steve said with a mocking edge to his voice.

Lydia's gaze flew back to his face and met the laughing persuasion in his eyes. She wanted to say, "Okay," but then she would be totally dependent on him. She hesitated.

Steve knelt down in front of her and took her hand in his. "Trust me, Lydia. You can't turn down a guy who has been in the kitchen all afternoon trying to prepare an edible dinner."

"I'm not dressed."

"You look beautiful to me. But I'll wait if you want to change."

"I—"

"Shh." Steve placed the tips of his fingers over her lips. "No more protests. I don't take no graciously or easily."

"I don't think you take no at all." Lydia laughed, her lips tingling where he had touched them. Suddenly she wanted more than his fingers touching her mouth. When he had left the night before, she hadn't realized until he had disappeared from view that she had wanted him to kiss her again. But he hadn't and she had felt a great discontent the rest of the night.

"Go get dressed." Steve straightened, scanning the room. "I think we chased Katie off again."

"She does have a way of disappearing when you're around.

"I'm not sure that's a compliment."

Steve smiled, the warmth in his expression touching Lydia's troubled heart. "Oh, believe me it's a compliment of the highest form. I think Katie McPherson is a matchmaker."

A sudden silence impregnated the room, and they stared at each other for a long moment, Steve's expression concealed behind an intent, probing look. Lydia ran her tongue slowly over her lips, trying to erase the scorching sensation of his steadfast regard.

He stepped forward, raising his hand, but suddenly he paused. His hand fell to his side as he said, "I'll wait for you on the terrace."

When Lydia reached her bedroom, she immediately made her way toward the closet, studying her limited wardrobe. There were so few of her clothes that she could wear because of her casts. Finally she selected a red sundress with a full skirt that wrapped around and snapped in front.

On the bed she struggled out of her T-shirt and shorts, but by the time she was undressed she was very tired from the exertion and the earlier therapy exercises. She started the laborious task of dressing. Her muscles were quivering from exhaustion when she was through.

In frustration Lydia pounded her fist into the padded arm of the wheelchair. "Damn! I can't do much of anything without a big production."

Lydia caught her reflection in the mirror over the dresser. Everything she was feeling was apparent in her expression, as if it were written in bold black letters for the world to see.

Quickly before she lost her courage, she applied her makeup, trying to disguise the gaunt lines of her face. When she appraised herself again in the mirror, she was appalled at the pallor she had tried to hide with too much blush. Her eye makeup was too heavy in her attempt to add the sparkle that had always been there. There was so little of her old self left that she marveled at the fact Steve even wanted to have dinner with her.

Lydia wheeled herself into the bathroom and scrubbed her face clean. When performing she had always taken great care to look perfect, to present a beautiful image to the audience. Now, it didn't matter. She was far from perfect. In fact, she wasn't even whole anymore.

Lydia managed to pick up one sandal and slip it on her right foor, when Katie entered the bedroom. Then with Katie's help, Lydia brushed her hair back into a tight bun at the nape of her neck and put on some lipstick.

When she appeared outside on the terrace, Steve slowly faced her, his expression still unreadable. For a few seconds he was perfectly still, then he reached for her. When he scooped her up into his strong arms, his heady male scent engulfed her. Any other time she would have relished the feel of his arms about her, but she couldn't rid herself of the reason why she was in his embrace.

When he placed her on a lounge on his redwood deck, he lingered, his face only inches from hers. Their gazes met, then parted in silence, and he straightened. The warm reassurance in the gray depths of his eyes sought to soothe her, but as his gaze skimmed her face, all she could think of were her pale features and hollow cheeks. She found herself lacking.

"Would you like something to drink?" Steve asked.

"White wine, please," she murmured, breaking eye contact with him and looking toward the ocean.

With the freedom she desperately wished she had, Steve walked into the house to fix them their drinks and to check on the progression of dinner. The evening was glorious with the sun having disappeared behind the mountains in the west. A balmy scent hung in the air like a warm, comforting blanket.

Lydia thought of the bush by the ramp to her terrace. In the short time she had been at Jason's it had been transformed from an ordinary green bush into a riot of vivid red flowers, every branch dripping with beauty. Everything around her was growing at an alarming rate while she sat in her wheelchair, unable to even cook a simple meal. She couldn't even get through the kitchen door without someone carrying her.

Suddenly after all the weeks of holding her emotions inside her, she could no longer ignore the deep-felt loss. Her dancing had been her partner, her companion for twenty-five years, and now, like losing a loved one, it was gone. Her anger and self-denial of the truth were replaced with the realization that she had to start over and she didn't even have any idea where to begin.

As she watched a couple walking down the beach, hands clasped together, tears streamed down her face. She had only known one thing. *What in the world could she do besides dance?*

The couple on the beach turned around and began walking back. They looked so content, peaceful in the midst of this tropical paradise where the temperature was perfect and the nights were made for lovers. But deep within, Lydia was confused, her heart in turmoil. Once she had had a body that had done everything she had demanded of it. She had used it to express her feelings, convey her passion, happiness, sadness. She had taken for granted that she would always be able to dance on her toes, maybe not perform but at least dance for herself.

"Lydia?"

Through her tears she saw Steve standing near her with two drinks in his hands. His brows drew together, worry etched into his features. He placed the drinks on the glass-top table and sat next to her.

Lydia wiped fiercely at her face, but still the tears flowed unabated. His concern touched her. She wanted to be a whole woman for this man. She wanted to be able to walk into his arms, to cook him a meal, to stand by his side.

"Please don't cry, Lydia." His voice was a raw whisper as he lifted his hand and brushed the tears away. "Lydia, what's wrong? Please tell me." Again and again he caressed her cheeks with infinite gentleness until the last traces of her tears were gone.

"I was dreaming. That's all."

The tender motion of his fingers stopped and the unyielding look in Steve's eyes seized hers. "About what once was?"

"No, about what could have been."

His hand slipped down to clasp hers. "Why did you come to Hawaii?"

"I couldn't stay in New York with all my friends around while I struggled to walk again. They live in the world I lived in once. The whole time that they would have been watching me, especially in this wheelchair, they would have been thanking God that it hadn't been them. I couldn't take seeing them slowly withdraw—it would be so hard for them to handle my condition. I would have been a constant reminder of what could happen to them."

"That's a pretty cynical attitude, Lydia."

"But the truth. You see, we dancers dedicate our lives to just one thing. Take that away and there's little left." Her voice cracked, and she fought to keep it on an even level.

"But when you shut yourself off from everyone who loves you, you keep everything bottled up inside of yourself." Steve turned slightly away and leaned forward, his elbows resting on his thighs. "Take it from me. That's not good, especially when you're hurting so much. It just eats into you until there's nothing left to consume."

Pain roughened his voice, and Lydia was aware again that Steve was running away from something. Her hand hovered near his shoulder, then hesitantly she touched him, wanting to take his pain away. For a few seconds he stiffened beneath her hand, then slowly the strain eased and he sighed heavily.

"You sound like a man with the weight of the world on his shoulders."

He glanced around at her, no emotion in his eyes. "I have my problems as everyone else does. But that's not what is important here." He twisted about and grasped her by the upper arms. "What is important is you and what you're feeling. I want to help."

Lydia couldn't bring herself to say she wanted more

from him than friendship. They met at the wrong time. If only they had met when she had lived in New York before the accident . . . if only the accident hadn't happened, then she could have come to him complete, a whole person.

"Are you hurting? Are you angry? Are you sad?" he demanded, his hold on her arms tightening. "Talk to me, Lydia!"

She shook her head. "I can't!" The tears returned to cascade down her face.

"Oh, Lydia," he murmured as he pulled her to him, his arms about her secure and reassuring.

He cushioned her head against his shoulder and stroked her back. Slowly her control was reestablished and her tears stopped.

She leaned back to place several inches between them. "I don't usually cry like this. I'm sorry. I didn't mean for this to happen."

"Since the accident, have you cried or talked to anyone about your feelings?"

"No, not really."

"I'm a good listener," he said quietly.

The tenderness in his eyes tore at her, the appeal in his voice ripped at the defenses she had learned to erect after the accident. "I feel like part of me has been taken away and I'll never be whole again. I've lived in the dance world all my life. Without my dancing I feel like a nonentity, half a woman. It's possible I'll walk with a slight limp, a woman who used to float across a stage, dazzling hundreds of people with her ability and grace."

"Is that why you wore your hair pulled tightly back in a bun tonight? Are you trying to suppress the woman in you? Do you think the beauty in you is only because of your dancing? That to take that away there is nothing left? You don't give yourself much credit."

"But my dancing is like an arm or a leg. My dancing is me!"

"Once there was a time when I thought I had my future all planned, but because of family circumstances I wasn't able to pursue the career I really wanted. In fact, there was little time at the end of a day for anything except to fall into bed. I had to learn to do something else. I had little choice in the matter."

"It's not the same, Steve. You had something to fall back on. You went from one career into another."

His grasp on her arms loosened and he slid a hand down to wrap his fingers around hers. "I know our circumstances aren't the same, but you're a tough lady or you wouldn't have reached the height you did in the dance world. Channel that energy into something else. You'll think of a career that you'll want to fall back on."

"My life has been like a piece of fabric. Take one thread out and the whole thing unravels."

"No, Lydia. You just have to mend that rip in the fabric. You're not alone. I'm here."

Steve reached behind her neck and slowly removed the pins that held her hair in place. A mass of ebony curls flowed down her back. He combed his fingers through her hair, his eyes never straying from hers.

"Your hair is beautiful down. It feels like silk."

Those words, murmured in a husky whisper, deleted everything from Lydia's mind except Steve sitting so close that his distinctive scent was drugging her senses, erasing the memories that were haunting her, at least for a short time. The seductive look in his eyes made her feel like a total woman, and she clung to him, wanting to believe that above all else.

Steve stayed his hands and looked deeply into her. Cupping her face, he bent slowly forward and lightly touched her with his lips. Softly, tenderly their mouths joined as if they were testing the temperature of the water. It was warm, inviting, soothing.

Rubbing his mouth along hers, he whispered, "I believe you've always thought of yourself as a dancer, disregarding the woman. You are definitely a beautiful, desirable, total woman, then and now. You just have to start listening to the woman in you."

Her heart was beating so loudly, the blood pounding through her body as though she were in an echo chamber. She pulled back slightly, saying, "It's not that simple. I—"

His arms encircled her as he crushed his mouth into hers, no longer gentle but demanding, passionately aggressive. He pushed his tongue into her mouth, seeking, exploring, tasting. She felt the excitement before a performance, and the exhilaration of the applause when she had danced her best.

His tongue probed her mouth with flaming insistence; his hands stroked her back with questing praise. Her arm slowly went about him, tryint to insinuate him against her. His very essence scorched the core of her womanhood.

"I want to make love to you, Lydia. I want to show you how much of a woman you are without your dancing. Stay with me tonight. Wake up with me tomorrow morning."

The sensuous firelight in his eyes intensified and

cindered any resistance she had. Lydia caressed his clean-shaven jaw, the play of shadows across his face accentuating the strong angles of his features. Everything in her life seemed to have been honed for this moment.

The sultry air weaved a secure, isolated paradise about them, lush with passions, torrid with needs. Lydia couldn't deny the woman in her who yearned for this man to love her, to make her whole again.

Brushing her fingers over his lips, she traced the outline of his mouth, then moved her hand behind him to pull him to her. She kissed him with a fiery impatience, thrusting her tongue between his lips to seek, explore, and taste of him.

Her thoughts were centered totally on him: his tactile warmth that burned through their clothing, the roughened feel of his hands on her back, his tantalizing scent that rivaled the heavenly tropical smells drifting on the winds. She felt like a flower on a tropical bush. Steve had become her sun, soil, and water, encouraging her to open up to his tender ministrations.

"I hope that answer's a yes," he drawled, standing then bending over to pick her up. "I don't think I could take a no."

"As a dancer I've always felt body language speaks louder and clearer than words. Listen to what I say." Lydia captured his face and drew his mouth down onto hers. He slanted his head to better fit his mouth to her lips, the kiss deepening and escalating with ravishing abandon.

Without breaking apart, Steve placed his arms under her legs and back, then lifted her up to lie securely against his chest. "Darling, I like your body language."

He chuckled softly, his chest rumbling with warm laughter.

Deftly he slid the glass door open with his elbow, then proceeded with long, sure strides toward the bedroom. For a fleeting moment Lydia was conscious of the casts on her leg and arm that made it necessary for him to carry her wherever she wanted to go. She frowned.

Steve paused in the doorway. "Your body is speaking again and I don't like the message I'm receiving. Let go, Lydia. Don't think of the past or of the future, only of the moment."

Her frown dissolved under his ardent regard. "When you look at me like that it's hard to ignore the moment or you."

"Oh, I hope you never ignore me."

"Ignore you, Steve? Never!"

He laughed with a rich, low arrogance of a man confident of his own powers, sure of what he wanted. And she saw in his eyes that he wanted her!

He walked through the doorway into his bedroom and gently laid Lydia in the center of the queen-size bed. Then Steve sat down next to her, positioning one hand on either side of her upper torso.

His smoldering study of her features boldly indicated his intentions, his eyes like hot, molten silver. "I saw you dance once, but you seemed so much like the swan queen you protrayed, unattainable, remote."

She stiffened, her eyes round. "You saw me dance?" Pushing herself up on one elbow, she forced him to straighten.

The passion in his eyes slowly ebbed in the cool silence. "What person in New York hasn't seen you dance, Lydia?" No emotion was in his expression now, his voice calm and level as he continued, "When I walked away from the theater that night two years ago, I had a new respect for ballet. But at the same time I realized that dancing was your whole life—you might as well have lived on the other side of the world from me."

"Why didn't you tell me you had seen me perform?"

Steven winced at the accusing tone in her voice, the same as in his recurring dream. Why in the hell had he even said that about seeing her dance? The answer was simple; he hated the necessary lie that stood between them. But his timing was off. He should have picked a better time to tell her. For once he simply hadn't thought before he had spoken.

Steven shrugged. "It didn't come up."

Lydia sat up, aware that she was trapped by her casts and hating her vulnerability. "That's a cop-out."

His eyes hardened, turning a dark gray. "What good would it have done if I had told you that first day?"

"Then you knew who I was from the beginning!"

"Yes, I knew. I read the newspaper, Lydia. It didn't take long to put two and two together," Steve said in a deadly quiet voice.

"But—"

"But what? Did it really change anything? I respected your wish to remain anonymous. I let you call the shots, Lydia."

For a breathless moment they glared at each other while his logic cooled her anger. "You're right. It would have served no purpose," she murmured finally.

A wry grin played at the corners of Steve's mouth; his dimples deeply grooved his cheeks. "I must say I could have picked a better time to tell you. It just came out as I was looking at you and thinking about *Swan Lake*. You were a beautiful Odette but the beauty I see before me now is much more real and touchable. There's so much you have to give, Lydia. Put your passionate zeal for life into something else."

"Hold me, Steve. I need to feel wanted, desired."

Steve gathered her to him, his arms a tight, comforting band about her. "I want you. I desire you, Lydia. There's no doubt about that. You have something special that enhanced your dancing, a love of life. Grasp onto that love and don't let go. It will get you through the tough times ahead."

For a long time Lydia clung to Steve, drawing from him the courage she needed to do what he asked. She had been running from life, hiding out. But there would come a time she would have to face her situation if she were going to have any kind of future.

His lips played along her neck, his hands caressed the length of her back. He bit enticingly at her ear while murmuring, "You are a beautiful woman, Lydia. Believe that."

He made her feel beautiful even though she had looked into the mirror earlier that evening and had seen a ghost of what she had once been. He made her feel cherished, special, and she smiled, a smile that came from deep within.

Gently Steve pushed her back onto the bed, his hands moving to unsnap her sundress, the cotton material parting in front to reveal her breasts. Lydia took pleasure in watching the male appreciation flared in his gaze. All traces of reality were swept from her mind.

In slow motion he touched first one breast then the other, circling her nipples with feather light caresses. Her breathing became shallow as he took a nipple into his mouth and sucked. She moaned, craving more as his tongue flicked across her heated flesh.

Lifting his head, he raised his eyes to reestablish visual contact with her. He watched her for a moment, his eyes absorbing the heightened excitement on her face, before he slowly lowered his head to kiss her mouth. Their kiss was one of desperation and hunger, as if they poured everything they were into it and in turn demanded everything the other was.

When the savage onslaught of his mouth softened, he whispered against her lips, "You have so much passion in you. So much fire."

Their ragged breaths merged in the small space between them; their heartbeats equaled the fast pace of the other. Again they watched each other as if they couldn't get enough. Steve brushed her hair away from her face, taking a strand in his hand and bringing it to his lips. He kissed the ebony lock tenderly, his eyes still on hers.

Standing, Steve quickly undressed, then towered over her in his magnificent nakedness, not an ounce of fat on his lean, well-proportioned body. When he knelt on the bed, he slid the thin straps of her sundress down her shoulders and arms, then pulled the dress from under her. Next he slipped her panties down her legs and over her cast, tossing the garment where her clothes were lying on the floor.

For a moment he studied the cast on her leg, then as if he had mentally shaken his head, he returned his gaze to her face, desire clearly stamped into his features. But for that moment Lydia had felt a break in the mood and her passion receded behind a cool front.

When Steve saw the doubt-filled eyes, he sought to reassure her with his mouth and hands, roving boldly over her. Lydia's lids fluttered closed and she surrendered again to her senses, to the wildly exciting feel of his mouth on her breasts, her nipples hardening under his zealous attention.

She felt like liquid fire when he stroked her between her thighs. He became the catalyst that set free her passionate nature, always expressed in her dancing, that had been locked away since the accident. Now she was complete again as she responded with her own demands, her hands exploring every inch of him, her mouth tasting the salt and sweat.

When he covered her, parting her legs to receive him, she reveled in the hardness of his whipcord strength pressed into her. She clutched him as he filled her, all her doubts washed away in that one glorious moment when they became one. In her mind and soul they danced a *pas de deux* together, floating, leaping, spinning as partners who had known each other for years.

Moving off Lydia, Steve lay next to her, his chest rising and falling rapidly. It took several moments for both of them to bring themselves under control enough to speak rationally.

"By now, you know, the dinner is ruined," Steve said with a laugh.

"I'm not very hungry anyway."

"Neither am I."

They turned their heads to look at each other and

burst out laughing. Just as suddenly as they started laughing, they ceased, Steve bringing his hand up to touch her cheek with a gentle caress.

"I suppose you should at least turn off the stove or oven," Lydia whispered in a breathless voice, the desire in Steve's eyes undermining all rational thought.

"Yes, I suppose I should." He rolled over onto his side, propped himself up on an elbow and faced her, his long length pressed against hers. "Later."

Again he made her feel whole, the woman she once had been, alive, passionate, fiery. In his embrace she expressed her feelings with her body again.

Later, after Steve had covered her with a sheet, he finally left to check on the dinner. He returned with a tray and placed it on the bed between them.

"This isn't quite the gourmet dinner I had wanted to impress you with."

To Lydia the cheese and crackers and sliced pine-apple and melon were heavenly as they took turns feeding each other, laughing, sharing in an intimacy that she hadn't known existed. A personal relationship had never been high on her list of priorities and now she was discovering what she had been missing.

After dinner Steve put the tray on the dresser, then lay down beside her and held her to him. She fell asleep in his arms, content and peaceful as the lovers on the beach earlier that evening had looked.

The jarring ring of the phone awakened Steven with a jolt. He slipped his arm out from under Lydia and quickly answered it. "Yes," he muttered as he glanced at the bedside clock which read five o'clock.

"Steven, this is Tyler."

Instantly alert, he sat up, placing his feet on the carpet. "What's happened?"

"You have to return immediately to New York. The Paris deal is falling apart. They want to back out. Yesterday they were ready to sign. Today they aren't. You'd better handle this."

Steven glanced over his shoulder at Lydia who was rousing from her sleep. Damn, this had to be the worst timing. How was he ever going to explain this to Lydia?

"Okay, I'll be there as soon as I can. See if Eric can be of any help." Steven hung up the phone, his thoughts racing.

Steve's deep voice, full of concern, pierced her sleep-shrouded mind and Lydia slowly awakened. Having replaced the receiver, Steve was staring at the floor, his back rigid. She reached out and laid her hand on his shoulder, feeling the tension.

Steve twisted about and grasped her hand. "I have to leave."

Lydia's throat closed. She said nothing.

"I'll be back, Lydia. I hope I only have to be gone a few days." He rose and walked to the closet. After selecting a suit, he faced her again. "I didn't mean for this to happen. There's an emergency at the company I work at and I'm the only one who can fix it."

Lydia sat up, holding the sheet up over her breasts. "What do you do for a living, Steve?"

Without any hesitation, he answered, "I manage a pharmaceutical company." It wasn't exactly a lie, but it wasn't the complete truth either. His tone didn't encourage any further discussion.

He picked up her discarded clothing and handed

them to her. "I'll help you get dressed and carry you back home."

"No," she instantly replied, then in a quieter voice continued, "You go on and get ready. I can manage without your help."

He stared down at her for a moment, indecision in his eyes.

"Please, Steve."

"I'll take my shower while you dress." He didn't think he could handle watching her struggle into her clothing. He turned away and strode into the bathroom.

Lydia waited until the door was closed before she started dressing. The whole time she was putting her clothes on she couldn't help but feel abandoned by Steve. Logically she knew he had to return to New York for business reasons, but emotionally she had come to depend on him and felt as if she were floundering in the ocean outside his house, trying to stay afloat all the while her casts were weighing her down.

When he returned to the bedroom, clad only in his trousers, and shrugged into his shirt, Lydia wondered what would happen if he didn't come back to Kauai. She thought she had experienced all the pain she could bear in the past six weeks, but a new hurt was added when she thought of not seeing Steve ever again.

Chapter Seven

Only one desk lamp was turned on in the spacious office. The massive oak desk was cluttered with folders and stacks of paper. A half-eaten sandwich lay on its wooden top next to cold coffee in a paper cup from the deli across the street. Beyond the large picture window were the bright lights of New York City, and glimpses of a clear spring night could be seen between the towering skyscrapers.

With his feet crossed and propped up on his desk, Steven was lying back in his chair, his eyes closed in sleep. Restlessly he shook his head, his eyes bolting open to the dimness of his office. He swung his feet to the floor and slowly straightened.

He ran the side of his index finger along his forehead as his heartbeat calmed to a sedate pace. The dream had changed; now, after the ballet, Lydia was shouting his real name at him over and over, pounding her fists into his chest. He had to tell her the truth.

Then he thought about the night before when they had made love and knew he wouldn't, at least not for a while. Her anger would be enormous and justifiable. Looking back on it, he knew he shouldn't have made love to her; it was only complicating their relationship.

But when he had seen her crying on the terrace, his heart had wrenched with anguish. There had been no humanly possible way for him to turn away from Lydia in that moment. He had needed her as much as she had needed him.

Relaxing back in the chair again, he turned it around to face the picture window and stared out at the blackness of the night. He had promised her that Steve Wilson would return, and he would keep that promise. Lydia had started to talk with him and that was a step forward for her. He wanted to see her again! He had to see her again and couldn't risk telling her the truth.

Steven rested his elbows on the arms of his chair and laced his fingers together. If he were going to return to Hawaii in a few days as he had told Lydia he would, then he would have to work day and night to take care of this complication with the French deal.

His body automatically tensed when he thought of the deal. It was nothing short of blackmail! And he would be damned if he would let them blackmail him. He'd forgo having a plant in France if he had to before he would agree to the French company's new demands.

Wherever he turned lately, it seemed smaller companies saw Wintercom as a big conglomerate that could afford to pay for what it wanted. It was always a constant battle to keep Wintercom at the top.

When Steven heard the door to his office open, he twisted his chair around to face Eric, who was entering the room. Outwardly Steven appeared calm, but inside he was preparing himself for a fight.

"Even in this dim light I can see you've been enjoying yourself this past week. Lying about on the beach, brother, while Wintercom's newest expansion might go down the drain?" Eric eased into the chair in front of Steven's desk, his arms folded across his chest.

"Where the hell have you been, Eric? Tyler has been trying to reach you all day."

"Relaxing. But maybe I should take some lessons from you. You seem to be doing pretty well after only a week. That tan is impressive. Perhaps the same blood runs through us after all."

Steven leaned forward, gripping the edge of his desk. "Quit the bull, Eric." His voice was pitched at a dangerous level, low and quiet. "Wintercom has a problem, which means *we* have a problem, *you and I.*"

Eric laughed. "The sun must have affected your brain. It's never been 'you and I' before. Why now, Steven?"

"Because when this is straightened out, I'm going back to Hawaii. And I'm not sure how long I'll be gone." Even as Steven spoke, he was surprised at what he was saying, and yet he had no choice in the matter. He had realized that the moment he had made love to Lydia. He had made a commitment to her to help her through the next weeks and he wouldn't back out of that. It suddenly was very important to him that he didn't.

"What's so important in Hawaii?"

"Nothing that concerns you," Steven answered coolly.

"If I didn't know any better, I would think we were talking about a woman. But you're probably thinking of expanding Wintercom to Hawaii next." Eric unfolded his arms and withdrew a notepad and a pen from the inside pocket of his coat. "What do you want me to do?"

Steven didn't say anything for a minute. He had been momentarily surprised at Eric's actions, as if his brother had finally come prepared to work. Steven decided to take a gamble. "I want you to go over the preliminary reports we compiled before we decided on the locations of our expansion in Europe. Come up with the three best alternative locations for our needs. I have to have this report in twenty-four hours or less if possible. I'm going to exert my own kind of pressure."

"The Paris facilities were, of course, the best ones suited for our needs, but the plants in Austria and Spain that we looked at could be adapted with minimal outlay." Eric stood to leave, pocketing his notepad.

"Eric, you'll have to stick close to Wintercom until this blows over."

Eric frowned. "For once you decided to give me some real work to do. Why did you have to spoil it by saying that? I certainly can't do this report from Long Island. Steven, I'm as much a part of Wintercom as you. It's my heritage, too. When will you realize that?"

Steven rose. Lately he felt as though his lifestyle had gone on trial and at this moment his family was testifying against him. "I'm trying to. But you're going to have to earn it just like I had to."

"I don't think you've ever forgiven our father for dying and dumping a hell of a mess into your lap."

Anger hardened on Steven's face as the palm of his hand slammed into the desk top. "I gave up a lot so you could go to college. How did you repay me? You got kicked out of three colleges before I finally found one that would keep you long enough to give you a diploma. Of course, that was after I gave them a substantial donation."

"I didn't know I had to repay you."

"That's just it, Eric. You think everything should be handed to you on a silver platter. You haven't had to fight for anything. Grow up and just maybe you'll be ready to run Wintercom one day."

"Why should I bother? You'll always be here."

Steven glanced at his watch. "You've already wasted five minutes. Time that we can't afford."

"Do you still want me to do the report?"

Steven eased back down into his chair. "Yes, and I also want you to put some feelers out to the three companies you come up with. Ones that can be heard all the way to Paris."

"Fine. I'll keep you posted as I go."

"Don't bother until you've finished. I'll be with Tyler working on an answer to their demands."

Stunned, Eric stood motionless for a moment before he nodded and turned toward the door.

"By the way, Eric, how's Mother doing? I may not be able to see her before I return to Hawaii."

At the door Eric paused, saying, "Fine, as usual. You're lucky you aren't around enough for her matchmaking. You should have seen the friend's daughter she fixed me up with last week. Boy, what a disaster."

Steven chuckled. In his younger days he'd been on several dates that his mother had arranged until he had insisted on no more blind dates. "Now you see why I claim I have to work so much."

"Maybe there's a method to your madness after all. I'll get back to you tomorrow."

As Eric was leaving, Tyler entered Steven's office and laid several folders on the desk. "I ordered some more coffee. It's going to be a long night."

"I think someone is leaking out information. The Paris company was satisfied to sell that plant outright until now. All of a sudden they want a share of Wintercom in exchange for the plant outside Paris. I have a gut feeling they've been informed of the importance of that plant to our expansion. This will set us back six months if we have to look for another place." Steven rubbed the back of his neck, the stress knotting his muscles and leaving him very tense.

"I'm glad the other two deals are completed. I've already begun an internal check, but this could be hard to track down."

"Good. Let's get started. Maybe we can call their bluff. I've offered them a good deal and I'm going to make sure they know it."

"This could take weeks to straighten out." Tyler stood at the conference table in the corner and spread the reports out on it.

"I want it settled in days, Tyler. I'm returning to Kauai when this is over."

"How long will you be gone?" Tyler placed legal pads and pencils before the four chairs surrounding the table.

"I'm not sure. At least three weeks."

"Will the same arrangements stand at Wintercom?"

Steven walked to the head of the conference table and sat down. "No, I want Eric to be briefed and put in charge of our new European division."

Tyler looked up sharply. "Are you sure? That's a lot of responsibility."

"I want to try it for six months on a trial basis. He'll be under close supervision, but if it works it might be the answer to his restlessness. This will be his, something he can set up from the beginning. You know, Tyler, when he did attend classes at the university, he made good grades."

There was a rap at the door, then two men entered the office and took their places at the conference table.

"Now, that Al and Bruce are here, we need to get down to business. Bruce, how do we stand financially if we give in to their demands for a piece of the action?" Steven doodled on his paper while he listened to the vice president of finance's report.

Lydia sat in her wheelchair on the terrace with her eyes closed and an opened book in her lap. The warm rays of the sun bathed her upturned face; it felt good to sit out in the sun. After Steve had left for New York, she had decided to do something about her pale features. She wanted to look good when he came back to Kauai.

She was scared to think beyond the moment. But the question was always there in the back of her mind— what if he didn't return? It had been four days and she still hadn't heard a word from him.

The first day of waiting hadn't been too bad because she had expected him to call. But by the third day, she kept wondering why she had opened up to a man she hardly knew and trusted him with so much of herself when she had turned away from her friends in New York.

"Lydia, there's a phone call for you," Katie announced from the doorway leading into the house.

"Who is it?" Lydia asked with anticipation. Shielding her eyes from the glare of the sun, Lydia looked toward Katie.

"Anthony. He insisted on talking with you."

"I don't want . . ." she sighed, "I'll talk with him."

"Great! I'll bring the phone out here, then I'll be leaving for the rest of the day." Before Lydia could change her mind, Katie hurried into the house to get the phone.

Lydia braced herself as she picked up the receiver. "Hello, Anthony."

"Well, it's about time you talked to me. If that woman had told me one more time that you were asleep or some other such excuse, I would have flown out to Kauai and personally confronted you. Well, Lydia Masters, do you have anything to say for yourself for this outlandish behavior?"

Laughter pealed from Lydia. "How could I? You won't let me get a word in edgewise. As usual, I might add."

"Good. You realize I haven't changed. I'm still your friend and employer. I want you back in New York working for me by the fall season."

"I don't know about that, Anthony."

"Why not? I've decided someone's got to take you in hand," Anthony replied sternly.

"You are impossible, Anthony. I told you before, I need time."

"Lydia," he said in a softer voice, "you will always have a place here in the company."

"We'll talk about this when I'm walking again, Anthony."

"Okay, Lydia. Everyone sends their love."

"Tell them hi for me. I'll call you later with an answer. I promise."

After hanging up, Lydia had a strong impulse to pick the phone up again and see if she could find Steve's number. "Don't be ridiculous. There must be a hundred Steve Wilsons in the New York telephone book. Why couldn't he have had an unusual name?" she muttered.

She missed talking with him so much. He wasn't like Anthony, overbearing, never listening to what she was really saying. He had so many interests, none connected with the dance world, while all Anthony ever thought about was the ballet.

Lydia leaned her head back again and closed her eyes. There was a part of her that didn't understand her reluctance to accept the job Anthony was offering. It would be a solution to one of her problems—what to do about her future. But Anthony, even though he was a friend, had a way of dominating the people around him, and whether she wanted to admit it or not, all those hours spent lying in the hospital bed had made her think about the person she had been. Now while in Kauai, Steve had started her thinking about the woman she had suppressed for so many years.

Something touched her hand softly, almost fleetingly. Lydia opened her eyes halfway and squinted at Steve.

"I was just checking to see if I should turn you over. You're pretty well done on this side."

Her eyes snapped completely open. "Am I sunburned?" Lydia looked down at her bare arms that held a reddish tint to them. She winced. "How bad is my face?"

"You see the color of that brilliant flower on that bush by the ramp? You're a close rival."

"That bad."

"I'm afraid so. Whatever possessed you to stay out so long? The sun here is a lot stronger than in New York."

"I've only been out on the terrace an hour. I keep forgetting that I don't sunbathe and my skin can't take it."

Steve moved behind her and grasped the handrails of her wheelchair to push her into the house. "I saw Katie leaving as I pulled into my driveway."

"This is her afternoon off."

"Now I call that perfect timing. I'm not back fifteen minutes and I'm already alone with you."

Lydia turned around and looked up at Steve who had stopped to open the sliding glass door. "Did you even bother to unpack?"

He smiled an outrageously sexy smile. "Nope. I thought you might like to help me unpack."

"Me? But—"

"You could hand me my things. You could talk with me. That house gets mighty lonely."

Inside the cool interior of Jason's house, Lydia still felt hot. She wasn't sure if it was because of the provocative appeal in Steve's eyes or the sunburn.

"Do like me—live out of a suitcase," she said. "When I was on the road, I rarely unpacked. There never seemed to be enough time for things like that. Now that won't be a problem. I certainly will have the time, and some left over."

Steve stepped from behind the wheelchair and sank into a chair across from her. "Do I detect a note of boredom in your voice?"

"When I was dancing and was so busy, I had a hard time even getting my hair washed. I used to dream of just lying around on a tropical island doing nothing but soaking up the sun. Now that I'm here, I would give anything to be in New York at a rehearsal. You'd think I could make up my mind," Lydia said with a touch of self-mockery.

Steve's lips curved in a travesty of a smile. "I've had those same dreams, too. But people like you and I don't know what to do with free time. You know there's an art to relaxing, I mean really relaxing."

For the first time Lydia noticed the gray circles of exhaustion about his eyes, enhanced by the irony in his expression. "Did you take care of the emergency?" she asked.

"I think so. I finally persuaded a company not to back out on a deal they had made with us. What have you been doing since I was gone?"

"Oh, sitting around." She flipped her wrist in a casual gesture. With Steve across from her, she immediately forgot the days filled with counting the minutes until he would return. Now everything was all right.

He studied her so intently for a moment that memories of their lovemaking made her shiver. She couldn't afford to fall in love at this time in her life. She was so confused, so unsure of what she was doing that she would have little to give to a relationship. Yet the memories of them together, not just making love but talking and laughing, had dominated her thoughts the past four days.

"This house doesn't have to be your cage. I have a solution. Let's explore the island together."

Together. She liked the sound of that word. It hadn't been in her vocabulary much over the years. But still she hesitated. "I have to stay in this wheelchair for another week, Steve. Maybe after that—if you're going to be here." She was almost afraid to say the last part of the sentence for fear he would tell her he had to go back to New York soon.

"I have a comfortable car and I'm strong, Lydia. Don't use the wheelchair as an excuse for not going out in public. You had a few bad experiences at the beginning, like in the airport, and you've decided it will always be like that. There won't be reporters waiting for you, or any fans." Steve took her hand in his and brought it to his mouth to kiss the tips of each finger. "I'll be there with you."

He spoke the last sentence as though he would be her shield against the world. Her world had been very limited and she hadn't even realized it. There was a strange kind of peace in knowing that someone cared enough about her to want to protect her.

"You have let that wheelchair trap you, Lydia. Please come with me." His voice was reduced to a seductive whisper.

"I'll go."

He bridged the distance between them and framed her face with his large hands, bringing his mouth down onto hers with suppressed needs. "Do you know how hard it was for me to concentrate on my work when all I could think of was you and the night we spent together?"

Lydia shook her head.

"Let's just say some people were getting pretty fed up with me when they had to keep repeating themselves. I think everyone was glad to see me go. They all readily agreed I needed a vacation."

"For how long, Steve?"

"I have quite a few weeks coming to me. Do you want me to stay?"

She nodded, her throat tight, her heart pounding.

"Then I'll stay as long as you need me."

He kissed her again, sliding one hand around to pull her even closer, the hot interplay of their tongues weakening any resistance. When his head dipped lower, his lips erotically caressed her throat, then moved downward as his fingers unbuttoned her shirt. She clutched at his shoulder, her head spinning from his dizzying assault on her senses.

"I've thought of this moment for four days, Lydia. I want to love you." His lips brushed over her breasts.

"Katie will be gone until tonight. We are alone, Steve." Her words came out haltingly, as though she had a hard time forming any coherent thoughts. Her hold on his shoulder tightened even more.

Steve picked her up and headed for her bedroom, where he gently placed her on the bed. Standing back, he slowly undressed, their gazes locked together. Then he knelt on the bed and undressed her reverently, worshipping her with his eyes. By the time he had removed her last garment, Lydia was aflame with desire.

She pulled him toward her and with a groan he ravaged her mouth with a driving hunger. Tangling his fingers in the black length of her hair, he explored her face and body with first his eyes, then his mouth, the slight discomfort of her sunburn forgotten in the mindless rapture of their lovemaking. His kisses, his touches plunged him deeper into her life, their union an exhilarating expression of pent-up passion.

Afterward, they both slept, content for the first time in four days. When Lydia awakened, the room was filled with the shadows of a dying day. The place next to her was empty and she quickly sat up, wondering if she had dreamed that Steve had come back to her.

Scanning the room, she found him sitting in a chair, a cigarette in his hand, a curl of smoke drifting to the ceiling. He didn't speak for a long moment, but instead inhaled deeply on his cigarette, then crushed it out in an ashtray.

His face was in the shadows, but Lydia sensed a withdrawal and instantly thought about his trip to New York. "Do you want to talk about your trip home, Steve? Did everything work out? Or is there some kind of trouble still?"

"It's nothing." He rose and walked to the bed, his voice crisp, his expression cool.

"Maybe I don't have a right to ask, but I know something is bothering you. Perhaps I can help you."

Help? He found himself getting deeper and deeper

into a hole, and it was going to cave in on him one day. He sat down on the bed, his back to her and murmured, "It's my problem."

Steven hadn't meant to shut the door so firmly in her face, but he heard her quick breath and knew he had hurt her again. Damn it, he wasn't used to talking to a lover. He couldn't tell her the truth—that she was his problem.

"I'm sorry. I didn't mean to pry," Lydia murmured.

Steven turned around and faced her. "I'm the one who should say I'm sorry. I'm a loner, Lydia. This is all new to me."

"Communication is a two-way street, Steve."

"Have patience. I've been traveling in one direction for a long time."

Chapter Eight

𝒟o you mind?" Steven held up a pack of cigarettes.

Katie shook her head. "Lydia should be ready in a few minutes. Our therapy session lasted longer than usual."

Steven touched the flame of his lighter to the end of his cigarette, then inhaled. Some of his tension left his body as he exhaled the smoke slowly. "How is she doing with her physical therapy?"

"She gets frustrated that she isn't able to do more, but on a whole she's not doing badly." Katie sat across from him on the terrace, looking straight into his eyes. "You know you've been great for her morale. Are you going to be here much longer?"

Steven understood what Katie meant. She didn't want him to ingrain himself into Lydia's life, then leave at a crucial time during her recovery. "Yes."

"The cast on her arm will be removed next week and it isn't going to be easy to teach her to walk on crutches, especially since her wrist will still be weak. And once the cast is off it will be painful to strengthen her arm muscles that have been locked into one position for so long."

Steven finished his cigarette and put it out in the ashtray on the redwood table. "Is there anything I can do to help?"

"Be there as a support. There's a lot going on inside Lydia. Up until yesterday she wouldn't accept any calls from her friends. And until you came back, she wouldn't go out of this house except to sit on the deck."

He could be there as a support for Lydia, but she would have to go through the pain and the frustration of learning to walk again herself. The one thing he could do for her, though, was rebuild her self-confidence. The day he had hit her, Lydia's image of herself had been destroyed like a sandcastle he had seen crumble beneath a wave. He could help Lydia construct a new self-image, based on herself, not her dancing.

"I'm taking her to Waimea Canyon as a starter. She won't even have to get out of the car if she doesn't want to. But if everything goes well today, I want to go out to a restaurant next week to celebrate taking the cast off her arm."

Katie tilted her head to one side and looked long and hard at Steven. "You see it, too."

"Yes. Lydia's afraid to go out in public and the wheelchair isn't the only reason. Her first instinct is to hide and bury her head in the sand. I'm not going to let her do that. She's a fighter and I'm going to make her see that." His voice was edged with the strong determination he was noted for and his eyes were the color of granite.

Through the glass doors Steven saw Lydia approaching the terrace, and he stood, ready to help if she wanted it. He forced a smile to his mouth, even though he hated having to watch her struggle to open a door and maneuver the wheelchair through it. It was extremely difficult with the use of only one arm. He constantly found himself wanting to protect her, to do everything for her, which would be the worst thing he could do at the moment. He knew Lydia was warring within herself, but he was, too. If ever there was a time he had to be strong, it was now, for her.

"Hello, Steve."

There was a slight coolness in her voice. Steven was determined to make up for the previous evening when he had cut her off about New York. There were times he felt as if he were walking a tightrope with no net underneath him.

"You might want to take a sun hat. We're going to Waimea Canyon."

Lydia's green eyes brightened. "Or I really will rival that red flower over there."

"I'll get it," Katie said, rising.

"There she goes, leaving us alone again." Lydia laughed, her gaze colliding with Steven's, a look of apology in his expression.

Steven took her hand in his as he leaned over and kissed her on the mouth, his tongue slipping between her teeth. "She must have read my mind. I've been wanting to do that ever since I saw you."

"Here's your hat," Katie cut in.

With his eyes gleaming, Steven straightened to take the hat from Katie and place it on Lydia's head. "We'd better be going. We have a long day ahead of us."

"Katie, since I'm going to be gone for the rest of the day, why don't you take that time off and do something you've been wanting to do?"

"The beach looks great. I think I'll go for a swim. You two have fun."

Steven began pushing the wheelchair toward the front of the house where his car was parked. "It must be expensive having Katie live in like that."

"I've never spent much money on myself through the years, so I've saved a lot. I didn't want to go to a clinic for my therapy. To me it was important I learn to walk my way. I knew the adjustment wouldn't be easy on me and this way I don't have to handle some of the emotional strain that would have occurred if I had stayed in New York."

Steven stopped at the passenger's door and moved around from behind the wheelchair. "You can't run away from the dance world forever. Your friends will still be dancing when you go home."

"I know. Anthony called yesterday and wanted me to tell him I would come back to choreograph and teach in the fall. That's an attractive offer, but I couldn't say yes. The word wouldn't come out."

Lydia lifted her head and gazed up into Steven's face, a puzzling look in her dark green eyes, the same color as the rich vegetation on the distant mountaintops.

"Sometimes I feel that more than my ankle and wrist broke during that accident. What's wrong with me, Steve, that I don't want to have anything to do with what I've always loved so much? Do you know how many dancers would give anything to be able to do what Anthony is offering me? And here I sit in this dumb thing"—her hand slammed against the arm of the wheelchair—"and I can't make up my mind. Oh, God, Steven Winters has messed up my life!"

Steven paled, his hand that had been moving toward Lydia stopping in midair and dropping back to his side. He felt as though someone had punched him in the stomach.

"Who's Steven Winters?" he asked in a whisper, barely audible.

"The man who put me here," Lydia answered harshly.

The color seeped slowly back into Steven's tanned features. "You never told me about the accident."

Lydia's eyes were round and dark, her hand clenching the arm of the wheelchair. It took a moment for her to speak. "I don't want to talk about it. There's nothing that can be done now anyway. If we're going to Waimea Canyon, we'd better be going. It's on the other side of the island." Her face was expressionless now, her anger in control.

Steve opened the door on the passenger's side of his sedan and positioned the wheelchair next to the seat so Lydia could transfer herself to the car. Then he put the wheelchair in the backseat before he rounded the front of the car and climbed in on his side.

Lydia stared straight ahead. With the key in the ignition and his hands on the steering wheel, Steve didn't turn toward her. The air in the sedan throbbed with disguised emotions, each trying to erect a false front for the other.

"If you'd rather stay here, we can, Lydia. What do you want to do?" Steve's question sliced into the strained atmosphere like a machete chopping into the dense undergrowth of the mountain jungle of the Na Pali Coast.

"No! Now that I'm in the car we're going." She twisted about to look at Steve, a pleading expression in her eyes. "Don't make me be stronger than I have to be. Play the male macho routine and tell me I'm going whether I want to or not." A smile gentled her expression.

He regarded her with a warmth that obliterated all thoughts except of him. She tentatively reached out and touched his hand on the steering wheel as though she marveled at the strength he possessed in that one hand.

"I'm not sure what I would have done, Steve Wilson, if you had kept on jogging by that morning and hadn't stopped to talk. You are a special man."

Beneath her fingers, his hand tightened about the steering wheel. His regard returned to the driveway in front of the car.

"I didn't mean to embarrass you or make you feel any obligation toward me," she said. "I was simply saying what was in my heart—no strings attached."

"Oh, Lydia, I wish I deserved what you just said. I'm not special nor any different than other people. In fact, I probably have more faults than most. My brother thinks I try to run his life and I do. I neglect my mother for work. I don't have the time for friends that I should. In short, I have been obsessed with my work. Does that sound like a man who is special?"

Lydia removed his hand from the steering wheel, her fingers studying it intimately, tenderly. "To me you're special. You came back to Kauai. If you were so obsessed with your work, you'd still be in New York. And if you're that obsessed, you wouldn't have felt you deserved a vacation in the first place."

Their clasped hands lay on the seat between them for a long moment. "I was engaged once to a wonderful woman who would have made a good wife," Steve finally said. "But I wouldn't stop working to give her the time she needed—we needed." He finally looked at Lydia. "I told you that I'm a loner, Lydia. I'm not sure I can ever change that. I'm not sure I'm capable of really caring for a woman."

He was telling her not to fall in love with him, yet she already had. The realization hit her with the impact of a ten-foot wave, emotionally pounding her against the sand. The bruises she felt were bruises of the heart. They had met at the wrong time in her life—and now apparently he was telling her they should have never met.

"Do you want to take me with you?" Lydia asked, wishing she could lace her hands together to conceal their trembling. Her cast stood in her way even for this simple act of camouflage.

Steve stared down at her hands, then up at her. "Don't put virtues in my character I don't have, and don't ever think I don't do what I want. I'm a man with precious little time and for reasons I can't explain, I have chosen to take some time off from work and I have chosen to spend that time with you."

He started to lean toward her, but instead, drew back and turned the key in the ignition. The car purred to life and Steve threw it into drive.

Confused, Lydia wondered about the vehemence in

Steve's voice. She sensed he had wanted to reach out to her but for some unknown reason had pulled back at the last second. He was a man who didn't give his trust easily. But somehow she would win that trust, she vowed, and settled back in the seat.

When she had traveled to the north shore of Kauai three weeks before, Lydia had seen little of the Garden Isle. Her vision had been clouded and obscured with anger at the fates. Now, through Steve's gentle understanding and probing questions, she was able to enjoy the drive around the south end of the island and actually see the beauty surrounding her and finally appreciate it. Sitting in the car as they passed through towns, Lydia felt safe from the tourists' curious stares. She relaxed completely in the front seat as they traveled along the highway with sugarcane fields flanking them on both sides.

When they started their ascent up to the Kokee State Park, Steve said, "Forget about what other people think. If you want to see the canyon below, we'll manage it."

"This may be a test of your strength," she quipped, but already the feelings of vulnerability were making her nervous.

Even the breathtaking views she glimpsed from the car as they wound their way up the mountain couldn't totally dispel her fears. She was trying, though, to master them because she was determined to see the Na Pali coastline from the Kalalau lookout.

Once at the Kalalau lookout, Steve carried her a few paces and pushed the wheelchair the rest of the way. The palms of Lydia's hands were sweaty, her heartbeat matching the thundering surf. But she made it to the top without asking Steve to take her back.

There weren't many people around, which helped, and, thankfully, the few who were there ignored her. At the edge Steve positioned her wheelchair so she could look down into the valley and at the coastline. The beauty before her made her want to leap to her feet and dance. Beauty always made her feel that way and the panorama of green-covered cliffs and azure-blue ocean was overwhelming.

Earlier when she had seen the Waimea Canyon with its similarities to the Grand Canyon, the red, almost barren-looking cliffs had reenforced her changing feelings. There had been a beauty in the canyon, but she had also seen the desolate loneliness—the vast emptiness of her future life manifested in the view before her.

Now though, the rich, fertile Kalalau Valley that stretched to the Pacific Ocean symbolized her past life. Lydia tensed, drawing in a sharp breath of clean, mountain air. It wasn't the people at the lookout she needed to run away from, but the view itself.

"I've seen all I want to see," she said in a voice full of tension.

Steve's hands lay heavily upon her shoulders for a full minute, and Lydia dared not look up at him. For some reason she sensed she had disappointed him. It was conveyed through the pressure of his fingertips.

"If that's what you want, Lydia."

"Yes, it is," she murmured, and the soft reply was caught by the brisk wind and whisked away.

He said nothing and neither did they move. Reluctantly she chanced a sideward glance toward Steve. His eyes held a look of exposed pain before he discovered her staring up at him. Immediately a bland expression fell into place; the pressure on her shoulders lessened to a light touch.

Lydia sought to explain, "It's not going out, Steve, that bothers me. It's this place."

Without a word he took her back to the car. When they were both situated inside and ready to leave, he faced her and asked, "What do you mean, it's the place?"

His question was unsettling. "The valley and ocean are like my life used to be—fertile, exciting, overwhelming at times. While watching those mountain goats along the cliffs, tempting fate with their aerial acrobatics, I realized I would tell Anthony no. I want to be out there experiencing the joys, thrills, excitement of dancing, or nowhere near it. Since I can't do the first, I'll do the second."

There was a crack in Steve's bland expression, a flicker of an unreadable emotion in his gray eyes. "You don't need to make up your mind now. You might feel differently later after you're walking."

Suddenly she felt calm inside, as one often did after finally deciding the answer to a difficult question. It wasn't the only question she needed to answer, but it was a start. She smiled, the calm something she had been seeking for weeks. She wanted to hold on to that feeling for as long as possible.

With a serene smile that represented her newfound peace, she asked, "Will you fix dinner for me tonight— at your house? I never got to fully sample your cooking skills."

A wicked gleam of pure devilment flared in his eyes, the tenseness of the moment before forgotten. "Woman, you might regret ever asking."

A look in her eyes equaled the playfulness in his. "I don't think so. I know exactly what I'm asking."

The wind softly whisked tendrils of hair back from Lydia's face. The scent of the plumeria flower from a nearby tree wafted to her and saturated the night air with its sweet smell.

The past week with Steve had been heavenly, making the time fly by until she could hardly believe that the following day was the day her first cast would come off. She was sure her love for Steve had been evident in everything she had done, and suddenly she didn't care that he knew she loved him. It was a wonderful, exhilarating feeling, meant to be shared with the world.

Steve slid the glass door back and stepped out onto the terrace, carrying a tray with coffee and two slices of a chocolate macadamia nut torte that was Katie's contribution to the dinner. When Steve had invited Katie to join them for the evening, she had just laughed and told them she could certainly find something to occupy her time. Lydia blushed when she recalled the knowing look in Katie's eyes. So Katie refused to stay around, but left a sweet and tempting dessert.

"Well, what was the verdict? Was the meal passable tonight?" Steve placed the tray on the glass-top table where they had eaten dinner.

"A few more lessons and you won't be too bad."

"Won't be too bad! I cooked my heart out and that's all you have to say?"

Lydia nodded, but her lips quivered from trying to

contain her laughter. A smile broke through her sober expression. He had carried her into his kitchen where she had watched him fix the teriyaki steak using a recipe from a cookbook he had bought to help him prepare the first dinner for her a few weeks before.

He had declared that reading a recipe wasn't any harder than reading a financial report. It hadn't been long after that rash statement that he had learned otherwise.

His gaze seized hers, the shared experience binding them. "I do appreciate your saving the day—or should I say the meal? You like to cook, don't you?"

"Yes, even though food, especially fattening gourmet dishes, don't go hand in hand with dancing. I suppose now, though, I can indulge myself with some of the whims I've held in check the past years. Once I fixed a chocolate mousse, then had to watch my guests eat it right in front of me while I clenched my teeth. Oh, boy, that was hard."

"You're kidding." Steve poured the coffee into the cups and handed one to Lydia.

"No, actually, in that case I'm not. I love chocolate and I knew if I had taken one bite it would have been all over for me. I would have eaten the mousse until I was sick. I have no willpower when it comes to chocolate."

"Mmm. That's something I will have to keep in mind." He surveyed her over the rim of his cup, his eyes pausing in bold admiration at her mouth for a full minute before he finally sipped his coffee.

A fire flamed to life in Lydia, and she was sure her face was flushed. As she took a bite of her torte, she knew Steve was watching her intently and her hand shook slightly from the tingling sensations his look always produced in her.

"This is delicious," Lydia said after several bites.

"Have you satisfied your sweet tooth enough?"

Puzzled by his question, Lydia answered, "Yes, why?"

"Good." Steve came around to her chair and took the fork from her hand. "Because I have something else in mind." He lifted her into his arms and cradled her against his firmly muscled chest before striding into the house.

After placing her gently on his bed, Steve sat next to her and cupped her face in his hands. They stared at each other for a suspended moment. Lydia felt the love she had for Steve well up within her and settle in her eyes. She knew little about his life, but it made no difference. She knew of his kindness, patience, and sensitivity.

Slowly his mouth descended toward hers, stopping a breath away. "I want to go with you tomorrow when they take the cast off your wrist."

"If they take it off. They'll X-ray it first and I might have to wait." A note of frustration sharpened her voice.

"If that's the case, then we'll face it together."

His lips, warm and inviting, moved over hers with a tender persuasion that she had come to associate with Steve. Deepening the kiss, he slipped his tongue between her teeth to savor the sweetness of her mouth.

While his thumb stroked the sensitive flesh of her earlobe, his other hand traveled lower, roving under her T-shirt and up to palm her breast. The erotic caresses of his hands worked a wild magic over her body, building one layer of passion upon another toward a peak of ultimate fulfillment.

As Steve slowly undressed her, she was vividly reminded of her casts. Scenes of her accident flashed through her mind: the seconds of fear and panic when she knew she should move and she couldn't, the impact of the car slamming into her, the blackness that engulfed her, and the hellish moment when she had learned she would never dance again.

She squeezed her eyes shut and tried to concentrate on the thrilling sensations of Steve's hands and mouth. But his light, rhythmic caresses ceased. Lydia opened her eyes to the banked desire in his.

"You're a thousand miles away." There was no reproach in his voice, only concern.

She shook her head as if that would dislodge those unpleasant memories. "Sometimes when I least expect it, I'm reminded of my accident. Please hold me, Steve. Love me and wipe those memories from my mind. I don't want to think of the past."

"I'll hold you, Lydia, but no one but you can come to terms with your accident." Steve drew her into the safe shelter of his embrace, her head nestled in the crook of his arm.

Her thoughts slowly became centered on the fact that a dynamic, special man was holding her, demanding nothing from her except what she wanted to give. In the weeks she had known Steve, she had learned to express her feelings, to open up the lid on her emotions, held in rein since the accident.

She was achingly conscious of every corded muscle that was pressed into her side. His sinewy hardness branded her skin. At this moment she was feeling a deep, intense love that she couldn't keep inside any longer.

Turning slightly, Lydia ran her fingers lightly over his bare chest. "I want you to make love to me, Steve."

He propped himself up on one elbow and gazed down at her. The smoldering, unmistakable desire in his gray eyes was a commanding aggressive pull on her femininity like the moon on the tides.

He traced the line of her jaw, the gleam of passion intensifying in the gray depths. "There is a lot inside of you, Lydia, that you have only just begun to explore." Steve leaned down and kissed her eyes, forehead, nose, cheeks, and finally her mouth. "And I want to help you explore them all."

His softly spoken words seemed to melt everything inside of her. His slow smile, packed with a potent male charm, produced a languid look of total surrender.

Parting her lips slightly, she ran her tongue over them, her eyes grazed with passion. He chuckled softly right before his mouth crushed into hers, the grinding pressure pushing her down into the mattress.

Her mind marveled at his tender touch. Her senses danced at his skilled seduction. Her thoughts revolved around his mouth that was worshipping her, adoring her.

With infinite gentleness he took her into the realm of mindless ecstasy where all logic was suspended. She danced again, soaring high above the earth as though she were a bird and gravity did not rule her.

"Lydia." There was a wealth of emotion in that one word as they came together in the midst of a cloud that isolated them from the world for one blinding, joyous moment.

As she slowly returned to reality, Lydia turned her head. "I love you, Steve," she murmured.

His arm that held her to him stiffened but only for a few seconds. It was so brief that she wasn't sure the movement had actually occurred. A thickening silence prevailed as the dark shadows of night poured into the room and claimed its domain.

Lydia had been so full of love after their lovemaking that she had blurted out how she felt. Now she wished she hadn't. Something was terribly wrong. Doubts that hadn't been between them for weeks resurfaced in Lydia, and she pulled away a few inches.

Steve rose and slipped into a short robe. As he stood at the window, the soft moonlight silhouetting his rigid frame, Lydia sat up and scooted toward the edge of the bed where she switched on a lamp. She had some things to say to Steve and she wanted to see his face when she said them.

With his palm braced against the wall, he twisted his head around in order to look across his biceps in her direction. His eyes were carefully devoid of any emotion, chilling her. His glance flicked over her before he returned his regard to the darkness beyond the window.

Her throat felt terribly dry, as if she had swallowed several mouthfuls of saltwater. In a weak voice she said, "Steve, talk to me. What are you feeling?"

"Guilt."

Her eyes widened. "Why?"

"Because I've taken advantage of you." He turned fully around to face her, and his eyes were no longer void of emotion. Within them there was silent anguish.

Lydia desperately wanted to get up from his bed and

walk to him. She wanted to wrap her arms around him and hold him tightly to her. She could do none of those things and she silently cursed Steven Winters for making it impossible.

"I wanted you to make love to me. I'm almost thirty. You certainly didn't take advantage of me." Laboriously she swung her legs over the side of the bed, the fingers of her left hand digging into the mattress. "Your lovemaking was the balm I needed these past few weeks. I needed to feel whole again, to feel like a woman, and you have given me those feelings."

Steve leaned against the windowsill. "There's no place in my life for a wife, Lydia." Raking his hand through his hair, he added, "There's very little time at the end of a day for me to give to another person. I would destroy your love like I destroyed Alicia's."

"I'm not Alicia, Steve. People love differently."

"But love is founded on trust and respect." He paused, searching for the right words. "That takes being together and getting to know each other with no holds barred."

"I trust you, Steve. I respect you. You have made this time in Hawaii bearable. At first, before I met you, I didn't know how I would make it through each day. Now I look forward to each day, knowing I'll be sharing it with you."

Closing his eyes, Steve swallowed with difficulty. "I don't want to hurt you, Lydia. I can offer no guarantees. I can't promise you tomorrow." He opened his eyes and looked deeply into hers. "I'll leave if you want me to. I would understand."

"No, I don't want you to leave. I'll ask nothing of you, Steve. And when you have to go back to work, I won't ask you to stay. I know I have no hold on you. I accept that." Her voice broke and she looked away. Biting her lower lip, she vowed she would not cry in front of him. For years she had been too busy to fall in love and now when she least expected it, when it would only add to the emotional strain she was undergoing, she had fallen hard.

The bed sagged next to her and one of Steve's hands touched her chin, forcing her head around, compelling her to look at him. "I want to stay. But don't expect something from me I'm not capable of giving. Don't give me qualities I don't have."

This time Lydia didn't look away but met his steadfast gaze with an unwavering directness. "If work dominates so much of your life, then why are you here in Hawaii? What do you do for a living, Steve?"

He took his hand away and stared at some point on the carpet in front of him. For a brief moment Lydia sensed a different man next to her. She shuddered and hugged her arms to her.

"I have my reasons for being here," he said in a terse voice.

The air in the room became static. Tense seconds lengthened into unbearable minutes.

Then in a softer voice, his gaze still glued to the same spot in the carpet, Steve said, "I'm sorry. I had no right to cut you off like that."

Lydia had pulled her emotions under control, her pride intact as she replied, "I'm the one who's sorry. I have no right to question you about your life. Now, since I can't do it without your help, would you please retrieve my clothes. I think it's time I go home."

"Lydia, I—"

"No! Not another word," she cut him off with both her cool voice and her proud, untouchable bearing.

Steve handed her clothes to her, then went into his bathroom to dress. With a quaking hand Lydia struggled to put on her T-shirt, underpants and shorts. It was never easy dressing with only one arm, but this time with her insides knotting in turmoil, she didn't think she could do it.

She fought back the tears that threatened again and gritted her teeth, resolved she would dress herself without his help. She was battling with the flimsy cotton T-shirt when Steve reentered the room, fully dressed.

He muttered a curse under his breath and closed the space between them in three, long strides. Without asking if he could help, he removed her hand and finished the task for her.

Their gazes met and held, a tether of strong emotions twisting and entwining about them. Steve sank onto the bed and gathered her to him, stroking the back of her hair as she listened to the rapid beat of his heart.

"Oh, my God, what have I done to you?"

"You have done nothing except to be here when I needed you. I owe you a lot, Steve."

He pulled back, his hands on her upper arms. They shook. "Lydia, even a man like myself, who works fifteen, sixteen hours a day, burns out and needs time to replenish himself. I had come to the end of my rope. I owe you a lot for being here."

His kiss was a tender seal. But Lydia also knew it wasn't a commitment.

"I'm a top executive for a pharmaceutical company that has been going through some tough negotiations to expand its facilities. I'm also the head of a special project overseeing the manufacture of drugs for rare illnesses or diseases at a low cost to the patient. Medical costs have been skyrocketing in the last ten years. I hope to alleviate part of the financial burden for some families."

"That's a tall order." Lydia outlined his mouth with a finger, then brushed her lips over his, teasing him with fleeting touches.

"It doesn't leave me much time for the finer things in life," he replied dryly.

"But you have the time now," she murmured against his lips, not kissing him but tantalizing him with her presence.

She parted and began to remove the T-shirt that she had struggled only moments before to put on. With a groan Steve again helped her with the top, then pushed her back onto the covers.

"You have such passion," Steve growled into her ear, nipping its shell lovingly.

"Will you watch the sunrise with me?"

"I will watch the sun rise, the sun set, or the sun at high noon with you." Steve took her mouth with a fierce savagery, stopping any further discussion of the sun.

Chapter Nine

Steven tossed back his head and downed the shot of whiskey. The drink burned his throat. A smile, full of self-irony, slashed his dark features and he refilled his glass.

He had had his chance the night before to tell Lydia the truth, but the words wouldn't come out. Instead, he had dug his grave even deeper with more half-truths. When she had whispered she loved him, it had felt as if someone had ripped his gut out. The feeling still gnawed at his insides.

He knew in his heart that he should have told her last night. But he also knew that when he did tell her, she would have nothing to do with him. She said she loved him, but when she found out the truth, she wouldn't. Her love was built on a lie, under emotional stress.

"Damn, what a mess!" Steven shoved his hand repeatedly through his hair, staring at the amber-colored liquid in the glass on the table before him as though it held some magical answer.

Have I made it worse by coming to Hawaii or have I helped Lydia cope? Is it better that I'm here, in spite of the fact she will hate me when it is all over? Steven wasn't sure he wanted to know the answers to those questions. Somewhere in the midst of all this was guilt and selfishness, tangled up in an obsessive need to help Lydia.

Glancing at his watch, he saw that it was time to take Lydia to the hospital to have the cast on her arm removed. Katie had warned him again that the next few weeks would be the hardest yet. He had to remain as Steve Wilson for at least those weeks, then his debt would be paid.

But the nagging feeling that he was putting off telling her more for his own needs rather than hers troubled him as he walked toward Lydia's beach house. With a firm resolve, he pushed the feeling aside. He had tried loving a woman in his life, but he had only hurt Alicia. Now he was going to hurt Lydia even more and he had already done her enough damage.

Steven stopped at a temple tree and pulled off two plumeria blossoms, the sweet scent permeating the salt-laden breeze from the ocean.

Lydia was sitting in her wheelchair in the middle of the living room, her eyes wide, her hand nervously twisting the fabric of her sundress. Every time he saw her sitting in her wheelchair, a part of him went numb. People in the business world swore they thought he was more machine than man, and when this was over, Steven felt that what they had said would be true. When he was with Lydia he was reining his emotions in tighter to handle the days and nights. But it was hard not to acknowledge that he had destroyed something beautiful, something the world had acclaimed and applauded.

Lydia smiled at Steve as he pushed the sliding glass door open and stepped into her house. He held out a plumeria blossom for her and one for Katie.

"Will you put it in my hair?" Lydia asked Steve as Katie walked to a mirror to tuck her flower behind an ear.

Steve grinned wryly. "You may regret this but I'll try." He took Lydia's tortoiseshell comb from her hair and used it to hold the flower in place.

The white plumeria contrasted and accented her long brown hair, which she now wore loose and free. There had been a time when it had rarely been worn that way. She was finding herself rejecting a lot of things she had once done. Her skin was lightly tanned and she rarely put any makeup on. Whereas before, there had never been an opportunity to sun, and often she had to wear heavy stage makeup.

"Mmm. It has a sweet smell. Thank you, Steve. It's just what I needed." Lydia drew in a deep breath. "Well, I'm ready . . . I think." Once her cast on her arm was removed, the hard work would begin. And when she was finally walking again, she would have to face the real issue she had been running away from.

Before moving behind her chair, Steve paused at her side, lightly brushing his finger down her arm. She shivered beneath the caressing finger.

"You won't be alone, Lydia."

His husky words promised her much; his look confirmed his conviction. She swallowed the tightness in her throat and placed her hand over his. She kissed his palm, the air vibrating with unspoken feelings.

Lydia looked from their hands to his mouth, lifted slightly at the corners, to his eyes that glittered with a silver fire. Time stretched into endless moments, and Lydia felt as if she were sinking into the smoldering embers of their gray depths.

Breaking eye contact with her, Steve stepped behind the wheelchair to push it toward the car. "I don't want you to be late," he said in a rough whisper.

"I should find out today how much longer I have to have the cast on my leg." Suddenly Lydia felt the strong need to talk—about anything so long as there wasn't any silence between them. She began telling Steve about her last visit to the hospital on Kauai for X-rays and the warm friendly people who worked there.

He listened patiently as they headed along the coast highway, but Lydia sensed his thoughts weren't totally on what she was saying. She stopped in mid-sentence.

Steve's glance flicked to her briefly. "Something wrong?"

"I could ask you the same question. Did something happen at the New York office? Do you have to leave again?" She forced her voice to remain calm. She would never show him how much it would hurt when he finally did leave. But it was difficult to keep her voice from quavering because she hadn't thought it would be this soon.

"No."

An unbelievable relief flowed through her, and she relaxed her taut muscles. Suddenly she looked forward to tomorrow. She wanted to savor each moment with Steve here on this idyllic island. The silence Lydia had been trying to avoid fell between them. She stared at the blur of greenery out her side window, her thoughts chaotic. Again the feeling that something was not quite right assailed her, but she couldn't help Steve because he wouldn't let her.

When they pulled up to the hospital entrance and Steve had pulled the car up to the curb and was getting out, Lydia felt as if she were a skein of yarn that had been wound into a tight ball. Inhaling slowly then exhaling deep breaths, she swung herself into the wheelchair. As Steve pushed her into the hospital, she placed her hand over her cast, hoping this was the last time she would feel the rough plaster.

An hour later her arm was free of the constricting cast that she had worn for so long, but any stretching of the muscles, not used for weeks, was painful. Steve had been by her side the whole time, through the X-rays and when the doctor had sawed through the plaster. The subjects he had discussed had run from global economics to his favorite painter. He didn't allow her time to ponder a single thought about what would happen after they left the hospital. He knew she was apprehensive yet anxious to get out of the wheelchair and onto crutches.

Outside in the car, the wheelchair folded in the backseat, Lydia whispered, "Only seven more days, Steve, and this cast is gone." She waved her hand toward her injured leg. "It will only be a matter of weeks now before I'm walking again on my own. There were times I felt this point was years away."

"When you're going through an ordeal, you either don't have enough time or too much, whichever you don't want." His voice was full of knowing amusement.

"I sense there have been a lot of crises in your life," she said, shifting in the seat to look directly at Steve.

One corner of his mouth rose in a half smile. "I've had my share, like the next person."

"From the little you have told me and the lot you haven't told me about your job, I think you have had more than your share. Is your job a high-stress one?"

The strong slope of his mouth turned down in a deep frown. The disquieting impact of his stare was unsettling. Her question had hit a nerve.

"Nothing I can't handle," he answered coolly, his eyes imparting that the subject was off-limits.

"Stress leaves its mark. I know. A dancer is under a lot of strain to always do her best. There is always someone who would gladly take your place in the company."

The tension drained from his face as he said, "I want to take you to a restaurant I found a few weeks ago. The seafood is divine."

"But . . ."

His gray eyes appealed to her, his hand slipping behind her to cup the nape of her neck. He gently tugged her toward him. "Their fresh catch of the day melts in your mouth. It beats my cooking any day."

His whispered words disrupted the pace of her breathing, the light caressing of his hand on the back of her neck sending her heartbeat racing. He lowered his mouth slowly toward hers but didn't touch her. Pausing a fraction away from her tingling lips, he kneaded the cords of her neck and shoulder, then brought his other arm around to encircle her within his embrace.

She wanted his kiss to brand her; she wanted to wrap her arms about him for the first time; she wanted them to be whisked away to a private, secluded place, not sitting in a parking lot—she wanted him!

Finally when she thought she would die from wanting, his lips came down upon hers, intoxicating her with his very substance, which seeped into her soul and took part of her. Molding her slenderness to him, he prolonged the kiss until she thought her lungs would burst from need of air.

But instead of parting, Steve touched his forehead to hers, his raspy breathing merging with hers. His arms lay on her shoulders, his fingers laced together behind her neck. It was several moments later before they were able to speak. When they were together, hot passion sparked instantly between them. For Lydia it was a new, electric sensation, yet bewildering, too.

"I'll go, Steve," Lydia whispered. "You are a most persuasive man. I hope this isn't one of your negotiating tactics."

He laughed, a rich deep sound that filled the car. "Hardly. I reserve this tactic only for you."

"Then you have mastered it quite fast."

Straightening, Steve started the engine, sending her a thought-shattering look before pulling out of the parking space. It didn't take long to reach the small restaurant that had a view of the ocean. Strangely, Lydia didn't feel uptight about going inside the dimly lit place in her wheelchair. The only person's opinion that mattered to her in the room was Steve. If the other people stared, she didn't care; she had eyes only for him.

After they placed their orders with the waitress, Steve raised his glass, filled with an exotic rum drink that Lydia had talked him into trying. "Here's to no more cast on your arm!"

Lydia laughed. "Yeah, and the fact I have to cover the rest of my body and then lay out in the sun to give my right arm a chance to catch up on the tan." She rubbed the pale, dry skin, fingering the line where her tan began right at her elbow.

"You could alter a few shirts. Long sleeves for the left side and half length for the right."

"Don't you think that would look slightly odd?"

Steve removed the little paper umbrella and pineapple slice from his drink. "I don't know how people can drink with all these things sticking out of their glass. I'm a whiskey and soda man myself."

Lydia angled her head to one side and studied him in mocked deliberation. "You know, you look like a whiskey and soda man."

"And how do whiskey and soda men look, or should I even ask?" He chuckled, a sound of pure enjoyment.

"Mmm. I think conservative, authoritative, and persuasive."

"Thank you—I think. That was a compliment, wasn't it?" He arched one of his eyebrows.

"Actually, I have no idea how whiskey and soda men are, but I think I do know you and you are all those things. And yes that was a compliment. You're those things and much more."

Steve exaggerated a sigh. "Good. I wasn't sure if you liked that type of man."

Lydia dropped her gaze to the plate in front of her, murmuring, "I like that type very much."

Silence.

When Lydia glanced up at Steve's face, he was staring out the large glass window that afforded a view of the ocean. A deeply thoughtful look was carved into his strong profile, and she had an impulse to smooth the creases from his forehead.

Lydia didn't want anything to interfere with the evening so she said the first thing that came to mind, "I called Anthony this morning before you came over."

Steve snapped his head around to look at her. "What about?"

"I told him I won't be taking the job he offered me in the fall."

A muscle in Steve's jaw twitched, but he said nothing. He continued to regard Lydia with an almost wary look in his eyes.

"I thought about what you said about changing my mind, but I won't." Lydia took a large swallow of her rum drink. "I may not know what I want to do with my life, but I do know one thing. I don't want to teach in the company. It doesn't feel right. It isn't me. It takes a certain kind of dancer to do that job and I'm simply not that type."

"Then I agree with your decision. I will be the first one to tell you that you have to be happy in what you do."

"Are you, Steve?"

He blinked as if he were stunned by her question. He didn't answer for a long moment, then he began to talk slowly, as though he were picking his way across a field planted with dangerous explosives.

"I never stopped and thought much about it. I have a job that has to be done and no one but me to do it. There wasn't a choice when I took it. I think, though, at first I resented it, because I had picked another vocation. Now it's my life. I guess you learn to accept when there's little choice."

"What other vocation?" There were a lot of questions Lydia would have liked to ask, but she sensed that this one was the only safe one to talk about.

"A classical guitarist." His eyes were carefully gauging her every movement, as if he hadn't discussed his denied vocation with another person in a long time and was unsure of what her reaction would be.

"Then we share a love for classical music. I love to play the piano."

The drawn lines in his expression eased and he smiled. "When I think about that other life twenty years ago, it's hard to picture myself as a classical guitarist. But I was good."

"Do you play now?"

"No," was the immediate answer.

"If you have talent, why not? For that matter, even if you don't have talent, why not?"

"Because I didn't have time for both in my life."

"Steve, I'm finding out quite painfully and rapidly that there's more to life than work. Life doesn't always follow the path you plan for yourself. You need to have interests and people to fall back on. If I had had that, I wouldn't be so lost right now."

Laying her crutches down, Lydia collapsed onto the couch, exhausted from learning how to walk with them. She hadn't realized until she had started working with her crutches how tiring the activity could be. And because of her right wrist having been broken, she had to use a platform crutch so there would be little weight bearing on the recently healed bone.

Lydia saw Steve at the sliding glass doors and motioned for him to come into the house. She was too tired even to get up.

"I see you've been at it again. Don't overdo it, Lydia," Steve said as he entered the living room and sat down next to her, moving the crutches out of his way.

Lydia rubbed her right wrist, the throbbing ache increasing from the last few hours' practice. "I had hoped once my wrist was healed there wouldn't be much pain. I was wrong." She winced as she ran through a few wrist exercises, a sharp pain bolting up her arm.

Steve glanced away for a moment, then forcing a smile to his mouth, he looked back at Lydia. "I'm sorry I couldn't get here sooner. I had a call from the office."

"This is your vacation, Steve. Don't they have anyone to do your work while you're gone?"

"It seems one of the people who was doing my work didn't show up this morning for an important meeting."

Breathlessly she asked, "Do you have to go back?"

Steve relaxed back against the couch, placing his arm about Lydia's shoulders and pulling her against him. "No, the meeting is over and they got along without me."

"Then why did your office call and bother you?"

"Actually I called them," Steve said sheepishly.

"Steve Wilson, this is your vacation!" she chided him in a stern voice, at the same time nestling closer into the crook of his arm.

"I know. But every once in a while I have a relapse and forget. I haven't called the office in over a week."

Lydia sent him a skeptical look that told him she didn't believe a word.

He held up his free arm, palm outward like a witness swearing to tell the truth. "Honest."

They stared at each other for a moment, then both began to laugh.

"I guess a person can't change overnight," Lydia said, laying her head against Steve's chest. "First, a person has to want to change, and Steve, I'm not sure you do."

His hold tightened about her. His breath stirred her ear, a tingling warmth spreading over her. "I'm working on it, but you're right. It won't be easy to change a lifetime habit," he whispered against her neck right before nibbling a path to her earlobe.

His tongue made lazy circles about the pink shell of her ear, devastating Lydia. Closing her eyes, she relished Steve's nearness. She wrapped her arms about him, ignoring the pain from the movement. When he had talked about the office, she was reminded that soon he would have to leave.

Fiercely she held him to her until the shrill of the phone parted them and Lydia had to answer it.

"Lydia, I'm not going to be able to make it to Kauai for at least another week or two." Weariness edged Jason's voice.

Sobering instantly from the sensual interplay, Lydia pulled completely away from Steve. "Why not? You and Maggie need to get away. You haven't accepted another gig, have you?"

"No." There was a long pause, then, "Yesterday I

thought Maggie had run away from home. We found her last night—hiding in the attic. Lydia, I was scared as hell."

"Why didn't you call me yesterday when it happened?"

"What could you have done? Fly home? I didn't want to add to your problems, but she's safe. I went to see her therapist this morning. I want to stay here for a while longer. Her therapist thinks we should meet together some more before we come to Kauai."

"Promise me you'll call if anything else like that happens. She's my niece. I care, Jason."

"How's everything going?"

Lydia frowned. Her brother was changing the subject, which was his way of coping with a difficult problem. He ignored it. Maybe she and Jason had a lot in common.

"I'm fine. I'm using crutches now and my leg cast comes off in a few days. So I will be able to walk to the door to greet you."

"Maggie and I will be there, Lydia. As soon as things are calmer here, we'll leave. I'll let you know when."

After hanging up, Lydia stared at the phone for a few moments. She was extremely worried about Jason and Maggie but felt helpless in her present condition.

"Want to talk, hon?" Placing his thumb under her chin, Steve compelled her to look at him. "Sounded like your brother was having some kind of trouble."

"My niece isn't handling her mother's death well. She's retreated into her own world and Jason doesn't know what to do. His career has kept him so busy over the last few years that his daughter is practically a stranger."

"Your brother should never have had a child if his career was going to be all-consuming."

"Steve, how can you say that? Jason loves Maggie dearly." Lydia moved away from Steve, angry that he would say that about Jason even though she had voiced the same opinion in the past.

"I've been there and I made the decision not to. Alicia wanted children badly. I knew the kind of schedule I had and knew there was no room for children in my life. It wouldn't be fair to them or my wife, leaving her with the burden of raising our children alone."

"Some people manage both," Lydia replied defensively.

"But from what you say, your brother hasn't."

"When Maggie was born, he wasn't the big star he is today." Lydia's voice had risen several levels as she squarely faced Steve, her eyes narrow, her jaw set stubbornly.

Steve smiled, a purely devilish grin, as he sought to erase the space between them. "I don't want to argue about your brother. I have one and I know how sensitive a person can be when it comes to family. It's okay if I criticize my brother, but I don't want anyone else to."

Her anger melted. It was hard to stay mad at Steve when he was holding her so close to him that she could hear his heartbeat, its tempo quickening, or when she could smell his distinctive male scent that instantly reminded her of their lovemaking.

"What time do you want me over tonight for dinner?" Steve asked, his hand stroking the length of her back.

"How about now? You don't need to go home."

Steve looked down at her apologetically. "I'm afraid so."

"Steve! You have work to do at home!" It wasn't a question because it was written all over his face.

"I have to make a few telephone calls and do some paperwork that won't take long."

She playfully punched him in the arm. "You're hopeless. Dinner will be at seven. Come whenever you're through."

"I knew you would understand."

Steve gave her a quick, hard kiss on the mouth and started to stand, then changed his mind. He turned back and folded her tenderly to him, kissing her again. His tongue slipped between her teeth and explored the crevices of her mouth with heated impatience. His hands pressed her even closer to his male contours, the kiss lengthening into a wild ravishment. When he did finally part and rise, Lydia was dazed by the mastery of his possession. As he walked to the sliding glass doors, she wondered what she was going to do when he took off for New York again.

Outside, the fiery heat of the day engulfed him. Striding toward his house with a frown engraved in his forehead, he tried to decide whom he would call first. Eric had left New York the previous evening for some unknown vacation when he needed to be in the office to conduct the planning of the European expansion if he were going to head that division. Damn, why in the hell had he listened to his mother and given Eric the responsibilities for that area? When he located his brother, he would have a few choice words to say to him.

Steven paused on his terrace, glancing upward. Dark clouds were rolling rapidly in and collecting around the mountains near his beach house. The peaks were obscured from his view. There would be a storm soon. Perhaps the rain would cool things off inside as well as outside.

Stepping into his house, Steven headed for the telephone, only to come to an abrupt halt halfway across the living room. With a smug smile on his face, Eric was seated in a chair, completely at home with his legs casually crossed and a drink in his hand.

"Well, it's about time you returned, brother. Visiting your little ballerina?"

Chapter Ten

The contemptuous way Eric had said "your little ballerina" hung in the air between the two brothers. Somewhere over the past few months Steven felt he had lost some of his famous control because at the moment he wanted very much to hit his own brother. Slowly Steven counted to ten, his teeth grinding together to keep from saying something he would regret later.

Eric uncrossed his long legs, placed his drink on the table next to him, and removed a pack of cigarettes from the top pocket of his casual knit shirt.

The action prompted Steven to ask, "On vacation?"

"No, just paying a little visit to my banker. I need a loan."

"When haven't you? Instead, I think you need a course in how to handle your money," Steven countered sarcastically.

"Oh, but if anyone knows how lousy I am at studying, it's you, brother dear."

Eric's relaxed pose was gone and in its place was a predatory stance. His brother had come to Kauai to settle a score, Steven realized with a weariness born from too much fighting between them. Steven found himself having to keep an even closer rein on his temper as he moved to sit down across from Eric.

"I need twenty-five thousand dollars, Steven."

"Why?"

"Does it matter? You've never asked before. Why now?"

"Don't answer my question with a question." Steven leaned forward, his elbows on his knees, his hands laced tightly together. His sharp gaze bored into his brother. "It matters now, Eric. Why?"

"The usual. Too much high living." Eric waved his hand in the air as though to dismiss the subject as irrelevant and unimportant.

But Steven could discern something akin to desperation beneath Eric's calmly feigned surface. "I don't buy that. You don't live that high."

Eric's face contorted into a scowl. "It's none of your business. Just give me the money and I'll be leaving this paradise."

"No."

"What do you mean, no?" Eric demanded.

"Just that. No, I won't give you another cent. You're on your own from now on, Eric. I'm through coming to your rescue every time you get into any trouble. Grow up and earn your own way for a change."

"I need the money." Eric pleaded, clearly panicked.

"Why?"

"Isn't it enough that I need the money?"

"No." Steven stood and walked toward the bar. He had to keep moving or he knew he would explode. Eric wasn't ever going to change. All he was to his brother was a free meal ticket.

"Then I think Miss Lydia Masters would be interested in knowing whom she is seeing. Don't you, Steven Winters, or is it Steve Wilson?"

The question halted Steven's movements. His jaw locked into a menacing line that didn't even begin to indicate his inner rage. Slowly he turned toward his brother, the icy look of disdain impaling Eric. Steven's purposeful movements were calculated to convey the dangerous power in him when angered.

"That was a mistake, Eric," Steven said in a lethally quiet voice that his brother had to strain to hear.

Eric flinched at Steven's tone of voice, but he recovered quickly. "No, Steven, it was your mistake. You're the one who hit Lydia Masters with your sports car, not me. And you're the one who came to Hawaii and paraded himself before her using another name, not me. My big brother has finally made a mistake. I never thought I would live to see the day."

Steven clenched and unclenched his hands at his sides. Over and over he repeated the action until he thought he had enough control to speak in a calm voice. "How did you find out why I was in Kauai?"

Eric crossed his legs, seemingly relaxed and composed as if they were discussing a mundane subject like the weather. "I became extremely suspicious when you extended your vacation so long and no one knew where you were exactly. That is, except your good friend, Tyler. I looked in his desk and came up with this number. With a little detective work the answers to the puzzle became clear to me. And here I am. I want twenty-five thousand dollars for my silence." Eric took a cigarette from the pack he had removed earlier and lit it. Smiling triumphantly up at Steven, he held the pack out in front of him and asked, "Oh, would you like a cigarette, brother?"

Steven ignored the mocking question and pivoted toward the bar. He fixed himself a whiskey and soda, declining to ask Eric if he would like a drink. His hands quaked as he poured the liquor into a glass and he silently cursed his brother. He would not be blackmailed!

Steven knew Lydia would have to be told the truth soon, but he had wanted it to come from him, not someone like his brother. He wanted to explain, but once she heard who he was she wouldn't listen to an explanation. His only chance was to tell her himself.

Steven took several long sips on his drink, buying some thinking time. He measured his brother over the rim of his glass and wondered what kind of mess Eric was in. It would be simple to write a check for twenty-five thousand dollars and send Eric on his way. But he couldn't do it. It went against his principles, which had been compromised enough lately.

"I won't, you know," Steven finally answered, placing his empty glass on the bar, half leaning, half sitting on a stool, his arms folded across his chest. "Remember the French deal. In the end that company accepted my terms."

"I'm not the French company, Steven. Your little scheme is finished."

"If you breathe a word to Lydia, I will destroy you,

brother or no brother, Eric." Steven didn't mean it, but he had to make Eric believe it.

"You wouldn't, Steven. You couldn't because of Mother. I call your bluff." Eric's angry stare narrowed.

Steven continued coldly to challenge his brother with his steely gaze, his eyes hard as ice. "There will be no more free ride for you at Wintercom. That in itself will hurt a lot. You aren't used to working for a living."

"Like some people we know," Eric shot back in a loud voice. "Sorry, Steven, I don't care to eat, breathe, and sleep for Wintercom."

"I never asked you to." For a few seconds, Steven sounded weary. Quickly, though, he covered the slip.

Eric's threatening look drilled into Steven. Steven could see his brother was debating what to do. It was in his eyes, the cornered look. Steven felt a momentary twinge of sympathy, but it didn't show on his face.

Slowly Eric's expression changed to defeat. His shoulders sagged forward, and with his head bent, he hunched his back as he dangled his arms between his spread legs. "Then this was a wasted trip."

"If your only reason for coming was for twenty-five thousand dollars, then yes, it was wasted. But I will do this for you, Eric. If you return to New York and work out an acceptable plan for the European expansion within the month, I will give you a twenty-five thousand dollar bonus. You're the head of that division now."

"And I'm supposed to be grateful for that," Eric replied with scorn. "I'm constantly on trial with you, my every action followed closely."

"I don't want your gratitude. I've never wanted that."

Eric looked up sharply at Steven. "What did you want?"

"For us to be a team."

The knock at the sliding glass doors startled both men. They had been so intensely involved in their conversation that they hadn't noticed someone approaching. Steven's gaze swung to the doors and he inhaled deeply, releasing the breath slowly. Lydia!

As Steven shoved himself away from the stool, he sent his brother a silent warning. He prayed to God that this wasn't the last time he saw Lydia. It was up to Eric now, and all the years of battling with his brother leaped into Steven's thoughts with a bleak finality. A storm was brewing inside as well as outside.

"Lydia, what brought you over here?" Steven asked as he opened the door. It was hard for her to manage with the crutches and it took all of his willpower to remain still.

Lydia looked from Steven to Eric, smiling at his brother, before returning her attention to him. "I was practicing using my crutches and thought I would drop in and try to persuade you to postpone your work. Katie is shopping for dinner and I was going stir crazy. I'm sorry if I interrupted something."

"No, that's fine. Come in." Steven moved out of Lydia's way, his attention riveted upon his brother, who was now standing.

Eric smiled the boyish grin that beguiled so many people. "I'm—Steve's brother, Eric."

Lydia sank down onto the couch, saying, "It's nice to meet you, Eric. He has spoken of you several times."

"Has he?" Eric glanced toward Steven, a cynical gleam touching his eyes.

"Are you here for a vacation, too?" Lydia asked.

"He's only passing through. He's just staying overnight," Steven answered, sitting again in the chair across from Eric.

"I'm afraid so. I have to return to work."

"Where do you work? In New York, too?"

"Yes, Steve and I work for the same company."

"Lydia, would you like something to drink before you head back?" Steven cut into the conversation, his body stiff, brittle. He felt as though there were a time bomb planted in the room and they were all sitting around waiting for it to go off. When Steven saw the hurt expression on Lydia's face, he hastened to explain why he was rushing her away. "I still have those calls and the paperwork to handle if I want to come to dinner. And it looks like it might rain. I wouldn't want you to get caught out in a downpour."

Lydia's gaze strayed to the picture window then back to Steven, accepting his explanation with a smile. "No, I've rested enough to head back. I can't get over how tired I got just coming over here. Eric, would you like to come over for dinner?"

Eric grinned, his impish glint not lost on Steven. "I would love to. Are you sure I won't be in the way?" Eric directed the question at Lydia, but his gaze was on Steven.

"No. My physical therapist, Katie, will be there, and you can round out our table."

Eric leaned back in his chair as if he didn't have a care in the world. "I'm looking forward to this nice, cozy little dinner party. Thank you for inviting me, Lydia."

Steven knew by the tone in his brother's voice that

his worries weren't over with yet. Eric was reevaluating the situation, and Steven might come out the loser.

Lydia positioned her crutches in front of her and pulled herself up to stand. "Well, if I don't get going, I won't have the dinner ready."

"Are you cooking?" Steven asked as he followed her to the door, wanting suddenly to gather her into his arms and just hold her tightly.

Her features were bright with a smile, her eyes shining with her love for him. Steven glanced away, pretending to busy himself with the lock on the door.

"Yes. I haven't cooked in ages. Of course, Katie is going to help. It's still difficult to maneuver with the crutches, but at least I can get into the kitchen now." She peered over Steven's shoulder at Eric. "It was nice to meet you. See you tonight."

"I wouldn't pass up this home-cooked meal for the world."

How about for twenty-five thousand dollars, Steven thought with an ironic slash to his mouth when Lydia was safely out the door and down his steps. The sky was darkening quickly, reflecting his mood perfectly.

"Brother dear, now I see why you flew all the way to Hawaii to see Lydia Masters. She's a knockout. No wonder you lied to her. If I had a chance to be in her bed, I would lie till I was blue in the face."

For a long, tense moment Steven stood motionless like a stone statue, his back to his brother. Then all of a sudden he slammed the sliding glass door open and strode out of the house, Eric's laughter bombarding him as he headed down the steps and toward the beach.

The rain, when it began to fall, was a welcome relief to his fevered emotions. If he had stayed in the same room with Eric, he wouldn't have been responsible for what he would have done to his brother. In the back of his mind, Steven knew his brother was lashing out at him for all the years he had felt that Steven had had the upper hand in their situation. For once, Eric felt in control and he was playing it for all it was worth.

Steven threw back his head and let the rain wash over his face, cooling his heated skin. The roiling clouds mirrored his confusion about what to do concerning Lydia. He knew in his heart that if Eric didn't say anything tonight, that he had to. This charade couldn't go on any longer. Tonight, one way or another, Lydia would have to know who he really was.

Lydia was in the kitchen, finishing up the last-minute preparations for dinner when Katie opened the door to admit Steve and his brother. For the past few hours, Lydia had been back in her element, cooking for friends, experimenting with different kinds of recipes. It was like old times and yet it wasn't. She wasn't the same person of a few months before. The love for cooking was still there, but the chef was changing, evolving into a different person.

Steve walked up behind her and bent over to kiss her on the neck. "Mmm. It smells delicious. And I'm starved. I forgot to eat lunch."

She glanced over her shoulder at him, leaning back against his solid frame, using him as her support. "Good. I tried a new dish with Opakapaka fish."

His arms went about her, crossing in front, while he nipped at her sensitive neck, whispering, "Whatever you fix, I'm sure I will love it."

"You'd better if you know what's good for you. Ever

since I left you earlier this afternoon, I've been in here slaving away at this stove."

"Do you want me to show my due appreciation now or after dinner?"

"Both," she said, laughing.

Steve released her and moved around to stand in front of her, framing her face with his powerful hands. He gazed down at her, saying nothing, imparting much.

"I'm glad your brother is only staying one night. I have a feeling I'm going to spend a restless night tossing and turning alone."

For a brief moment the hands on her face tensed. His eyelids closed halfway to conceal his expression. The mention of his brother had brought a troubled look to his eyes, at the moment hidden from her. But she had sensed it earlier at his house and now she was aware of it again. His relationship with Eric was less than ideal. Was Eric the reason he had escaped New York for a well-deserved vacation when it was obvious his work still held a hold over him? Suddenly she wished she hadn't invited Eric to dinner. She didn't want anything unpleasant to intrude on the little time she and Steve had left.

"I shouldn't have asked your brother to eat with us tonight. I'm sorry."

Steve opened his eyes to reveal the tenderness within. "The problems with Eric go back a long way." His mouth lifted slightly in a half smile. "He resents the hell out of me and I'm extremely impatient when it comes to my brother. I know what he's capable of and hate the waste. He has so much to offer if he would ever see that."

Steve's hands slid around to clasp behind her neck,

pulling her closer. "But frankly, right now I don't want to discuss Eric. In fact, I don't want to talk at all."

His mouth touched hers, his hands slipping down her back to press her into him. She felt the depth of his arousal and wished they were alone. A kiss was not enough. Where Steve was concerned she couldn't get enough of him.

She molded herself against him, hating the fabric that stood between them. She wanted to touch every inch of his naked body with her own. She yearned for the darkness of night to cloak them in their own private world. Instead, she had to settle for their tongues meeting and dueling, for his hands to move under her sundress and sear a path over her back, for the heat of his mouth to flame hers.

Someone cleared his throat and they broke away. Eric stood in the doorway, leaning against the doorjamb, a deep satisfaction in his eyes that produced an instant tension in the room.

Eric pushed away from the doorjamb and headed for the refrigerator. "I told Katie I would fill the ice bucket. She needed to make a call in her bedroom." As he placed the ice in the bucket, he continued, "Katie tells me this is your brother's house, Lydia. I'm an avid fan of Jason Masters. He's quite a performer. I saw his act in Vegas once and I must say he can put on some show. Didn't I read somewhere his wife died a few months back?"

"Yes," Lydia replied, watching Steve out of the corner of her eye. He was leaning casually against the countertop, but his alert eyes never missed a movement of Eric's.

"Oh, I'm sorry to hear that. But he's been performing a lot lately, hasn't he?"

"A man driven by his wife's death."

"Yes, I suppose, a man can be driven by a lot of things—like guilt," Eric replied.

Eric wasn't looking at Lydia but at Steve, a silent message passing between the two brothers. Lydia wondered if Steve was a driven man as she made her way toward the living room, the atmosphere in the kitchen stifling. She wanted Steve to open up to her and tell her what was on his mind; something was weighing heavily on his conscience.

In the living room Eric fixed everyone a drink while they waited for Katie to return. Lydia tried to lighten the tense mood but met with one-word answers to her questions from both Eric and Steve. Exasperated, she gave up and sipped her drink.

"Sorry it took me so long," Katie said as she reentered the room. "But my mother had to tell me every detail of my nephew's exploits at the beach." She came to a stop, looked at everyone, then asked, "Everything okay?"

Eric smiled, his eyes alight with a teasing glint. "Now, what could possibly be wrong? The dinner smells divine. There are two beautiful women in the room and anything you could want to drink. I would say everything is great."

"Good. I won't be but a minute. I'll get the dinner ready to serve." Katie started for the kitchen.

"I'll help you, Katie my dear." Eric was on his feet and following her into the kitchen.

The tension in the air deflated like a balloon, and Lydia sighed.

"I'm the one who's sorry, Lydia," Steve said. "This isn't going to be an easy dinner to get through."

"Don't worry about it. I'm glad you're here. From the little I've seen, I don't think you two should have eaten alone."

"Yeah, World War Three might have erupted next door." His darkened gaze seized hers. "Lydia, after dinner I need to talk with you."

"About Eric."

"No, about us."

Her heartbeat throbbed in her chest. "Us?"

"Yes, but this isn't the time nor the place." He indicated with a glance Katie and Eric in the kitchen, their voices drifting into the living room.

"I agree," Lydia murmured as Katie came to the door to announce dinner was ready.

When they were all seated at the dining room table and their plates full of the various dishes Lydia and Katie had prepared, Eric asked, "Is there any nightlife on this island? I thought before I had to go back to the salt mines that I would sample some of it. That is, if I can persuade you to join me, Katie."

"I've only been to Kauai once before so I'm not sure where the nightlife is," Katie said.

"Don't worry, Katie. If there is any, my brother has a knack for finding it." Steve's voice was teasing but the look in his eyes wasn't.

"It sure beats spending my nights working in an office putting in hours and hours of overtime." Eric raised his fork and gestured with it. "Do you know that Steve here would rather spend his weekends working at"—there was the slightest pause before Eric continued—"at the office than anything else. I'm not even sure he goes home some nights."

Lydia looked sideways at Steve, who was clamping his fork so tightly that his knuckles were white. She wanted to take that hand and stroke the anger away; she wished the time would speed forward until they could be alone.

"Come to think of it, I do know a place not too far from here that has a good band." Katie's brows were furrowed, the usual twinkle in her eye a speculative gleam.

"Great! Then eat up. I'm ready to paint this island red. Tomorrow it's back to work and no telling how long it will be before I'm let out of my cage," Eric said with a robust laugh, but his eyes didn't match the amusement in his voice.

"Cage? That doesn't sound like a man who enjoys his job." Katie's puzzled look intensified. "What do you do, Eric?"

Eric's eyes glowed with immense satisfaction. Steve started to say something, but Eric cut him off. "I'm vice president of nothing."

Lydia had had enough. Her dinner party had turned very quickly into a battleground between Steve and Eric. "Have you ever been to Hawaii, Eric?" She hoped that was a safe topic.

"No. But I enjoy the Caribbean when I have a chance, which isn't—"

"Oh, now, the Caribbean is beautiful. Different, though, from Hawaii." Lydia was determined that the negative undertones would remain suppressed. "Many of the Caribbean islands are flatter and hotter than here."

For the rest of the meal they discussed the differences between the two tropical playgrounds. Whenever the subject of their conversation was heading toward a dangerous topic, Lydia directed it back toward safety. Later, though, she was going to find out some answers from Steve.

After the table was cleared and the dishes washed, Eric and Katie left for the disco. The minute the door was closed behind them, the relief was like a cool refreshing breeze from the ocean. In the living room Lydia and Steve exchanged looks. Mixed with the calm in Steve's expression was something else, undefinable, but disquieting.

"Let's go out onto the terrace for that talk you wanted, Steve. I have a few questions myself."

His expression became completely closed. "I'm sure you do after the last two hours."

Lydia settled herself on the redwood love seat, expecting Steve to sit down next to her. He remained standing by the railing, leaning into it, his back to her.

The air smelled of the rain that had fallen hours before as if everything had been washed clean and was sparkling fresh. Hundreds of stars glittered in the sky, bright like diamonds, but the moon was absent. Suddenly Lydia wished she had switched on the light before coming outside. The setting was romantic, but she sensed romance was not the impending topic for discussion.

Steven stared at the water beyond the trees, listening to the rhythmic pounding of the surf that equalled the beat of his heart. His pulse roared in his ears, the hammering against his temples a pain that he concentrated on. It lessened the anguish he was feeling at what had to be done. Somewhere he had to find the courage to tell her and soon.

Turning toward Lydia who was sitting on the love seat waiting for him to speak, he postponed the truth for a few more minutes. With long strides he was close enough to stare down at her, thankful that she couldn't see the naked torment in his eyes. He wanted to relish just a few minutes more with her alone, nothing between them but the past weeks of companionship.

Taking her face in his hands, he bent over and touched his lips softly to hers. "You are special, Lydia. Do you believe me when I say that?"

"Yes, Steve, I do."

"Not because of who you were, but because of who you are." He sat down, his hands trailing down to settle heavily upon her shoulders. "That's important for you to remember."

He drew her against his chest and held her near to his heart. Closing his eyes, he sucked in deep breaths to ease the aching beat of his heart, but nothing relieved the pain he was experiencing, put there by the lie that stood between them. Nothing but the truth, Steve acknowledged. Then perhaps they could start over.

But still Steven couldn't speak. His mouth and throat were parched; his mind tumbled with a hundred different ways to begin, each discarded as quickly as they originated. He felt as if someone had ripped him open and had exposed his every thought and emotion that he had tried to hide for years.

"Steve, what's wrong? I want to help. Don't shut me out. I love you. Please let me help you." Alarm sounded in her voice.

Steven closed his eyes tightly shut. A steel band,

wrapped about him, was pulled taut, suffocating him, imprisoning his next breath. A warm caressing paradise encased them in a perfect background, but to Steven it was a gilded cage.

Lydia tilted her head up to look into Steve's face, concealed by the dark shadows of night. Closing the distance between them, she kissed him with an urgency founded in uncertainty. Her fingers were entwined at the nape of his neck, gathering him closer to recapture the feeling of intimacy with him. But an impregnable barrier was between them, and Lydia pulled away, suddenly very cold in the heat of a tropical night.

"Steve!" His name, torn from her throat, was a plea for some answers.

"Lydia, I don't know where to begin. There is so much I need to explain." His chest rose with the pause. "I'm not Steve Wilson, but Steven Winters," he expelled on a long breath.

Chapter Eleven

Lydia felt instantly numb as though she had been plunged into a river of ice. Her life sensations and emotions were emptied from her body, swept away in that one blinding second when everything had changed. The name Steven Winters echoed with recoiling vibrations over and over in her mind, and she relived that moment when Jason had told her she would never dance again. This man before her had taken the most precious thing in her life and had destroyed it.

No! It can't be true. This is a nightmare, Lydia screamed silently.

Slowly her anger dominated her feelings to the exclusion of everything else. Not only had he taken her dancing but he had lied to her and taken her love as well. She couldn't forgive him for that.

Steven had risen and was standing a few feet away from her. Even though it was dark, Lydia struggled to hide her pain behind a proud, aloof mask and strove to keep her voice from quavering.

"I suppose I should be grateful that you finally decided to tell me who you are." Her sharp words were like daggers, meant to cut him to shreds. "Well, pardon me, if I'm not."

"I don't want your gratitude. It seems today that's all I've said." He took a step toward her but stopped, his stance stiff, his shoulders set in an unyeilding line.

"Frankly, Steven Winters"—his name was spoken with such disdain that he cringed—"I don't care what you want. Didn't you understand from your lawyer that I didn't want to have anything to do with you? Nothing!" Her mask slipped, revealing her fury, directed at Steven with unfailing accuracy.

"Lydia, let me explain—"

"You certainly have some kind of nerve, I must say. Mr. Jackson told me you were a determined man, but I guess I didn't know the extent of your determination until now."

"Lydia, it's not like you think."

Steven moved with a quickness that surprised her. In seconds he was beside her on the love seat, pushing the crutches out of her grasp. Trapped next to him, she was so incensed that any foolishness she felt was eclipsed by her rage. Whether she had her crutches within reach or not, she wasn't going to stay there and listen to more lies. She started to rise when a set of steel talons clamped about her arm and held her prisoner on the love seat.

With an incredible effort, she didn't struggle to free herself. It would have been useless and she already felt like the complete fool. "There isn't anything you can tell me that will make things right. I just want to be left alone. I told that to your lawyer. If I had known what you were going to do, I would have taken your damn money. Is there some reason you enjoy hurting me?" When Steven began to speak, Lydia cut him off. "Don't answer. It doesn't matter. It would only be more lies. I don't ever want to see you again. You've paid your debt to me. Now, go."

His fingers about her arm bit into her skin and from the faint light she could discern the anger that lined his face. The image of a hunter, who had found his game, hardened in her mind and she looked away.

"You are hurting my arm. Please let it go." Each word was clipped between gritted teeth.

"I think you at least owe me a chance to explain after what's happened between us these last few weeks."

"Because of what's happened between us, I feel cheap. I trusted you and . . ." Her voice that shook with fury and anguish faded, and Lydia moistened her lips. Then in a steadier voice she added, "I just want to forget these past weeks and get on with my life. I can't stop you from talking, but I will not listen." Lydia stressed the words of the last sentence, speaking slowly as though to a child.

"Do you really think you can forget what's between us?"

"Now, that's an arrogant statement if I've ever heard one," she replied sarcastically, her gaze trained on the darkness beyond the terrace.

The hand on her arm loosened, but his other came up to force her head around, demanding her full attention. He caressed her cheek and she jerked back. For a long, strained moment he stared into her eyes, then his hands dropped away, freeing her finally.

"I want to explain. I know it doesn't change what I have done to you, but it might help you to understand why. However, I can see it's useless to try. Good night, Lydia." Rising, he walked away into the blackness of night.

Stunned, Lydia stared at his retreating figure. He had actually sounded like the injured party! She was the one who had been hurt; she had fallen in love with him, a love that was founded on a lie. She was the one who had no career.

She lifted a shaky hand to her feverish face, touching the place where his fingers had been moments before. She had told him all she wanted to do was forget him, but she knew she never would completely because she had never said she had loved a man before him. It wasn't something she would be able to forget lightly, if ever.

The breeze rustled the palm fronds, a sound like gently falling rain, drawing her toward the beach. Using her crutches, she pulled herself to her feet and headed down the wooden path toward the ocean. On the log under the giant pine tree, she sat and gazed at the incoming tide.

Focusing all her attention on the soothing sounds of nature, she cleared her mind of all thoughts. She felt insulated in a vacuum where no feelings were permitted to exist. Her rage had exhausted her body and mind, leaving nothing in its wake, and she relished the void.

Lydia stood, most of her weight leaning against the windowsill, and stared out at the gray dawn. Automatically as she had done so many times the past weeks, she had awakened right before sunrise. She had tried to go back to sleep, but even with only a little rest the night before, she couldn't. She was filled with unwanted thoughts, the void gone and in its place a parade of emotions and scenes flitted through her thoughts, all concerning Steve. Even now she found it difficult to think of him as Steven Winters. Lydia desperately wondered if this gut-wrenching pain when she unwillingly thought of him would ever cease.

Her hands tensed on her crutches as Steve came into view, jogging down the beach in front of her house. She shut her eyes to his powerful physique, but his haunting image still taunted her. Turning away, she couldn't understand her need to torture herself like this.

At the piano Lydia began to play a medley of brooding songs that reflected her mood. She remained at the piano for over an hour until the pain in her injured arm monopolized her thoughts to the exclusion of anything else.

Bringing the ebony top down over the ivory keys, she ran her finger along the edge of it, feeling drained emotionally but better able to cope with the rest of the long day ahead of her. Music always did that for her; it was an escape, another way she expressed her innermost feelings.

She heard Katie moving about in the kitchen and realized her companion must have awakened and was fixing breakfast. She had been so absorbed in the music that she hadn't known Katie had even passed through the living room.

Lydia was heading into the kitchen to see if she could

help when the phone rang. She stiffened, the shrill ringing intrusive.

"I'll get it," Katie called out from the kitchen.

Lydia stood motionless, waiting for Katie to tell her who was calling, a fact she already knew. Jumbled thoughts rolled through her mind. The aching throb in her arm was repeated in her temples.

"It's for you, Lydia. It's Steve."

"I don't want to talk with him."

"But, it's—"

"Tell him not to call back." Lydia turned away from the kitchen door and made her way to the bedroom. Somehow she knew his next move would be to come over and she didn't want to be anywhere near the living room.

A few minutes later Katie knocked lightly at her door, then called out her name before opening it. "He said something about coming over, Lydia."

Sitting on her bed, Lydia swung her legs on top of the crumbled sheets. The cast seemed to weigh at least five pounds more than before. "I don't want to talk to him or see him. You have to get rid of him for me." Panic mingled with her desperation. "Please, Katie, you have to do this for me."

"I knew there were some strong undercurrents last night at dinner, but I thought it was between Steve and his brother, not you two," Katie replied, concern and bewilderment interwoven in her voice.

Tears, held in check all the previous night, crowded Lydia's eyes. A burning tightness lodged in her throat. "Steve is really Steven Winters, the man who hit me with his car." Saying it out loud to Katie snatched away the last vestige of her shock completely, and the tears scalded a path down her cheeks and fell onto her clasped hands.

"Oh, no, Lydia. No wonder you're hurting so much. I'm really sorry. But don't you think Steve might be hurting, too? He didn't sound like himself on the phone a minute ago."

"No! He isn't," Lydia replied vehemently, as though she had to convince herself the truth of those words as well as Katie.

"He told me all he wanted to do was explain."

Lydia placed her hands over her ears and shook her head violently from one side to the other. "I don't want to hear more lies."

Even in her bedroom Lydia could hear the pounding on the sliding glass door. Her eyes grew round with panic and she pleaded, "I can't see him, Katie. Please leave me some pride and dignity."

"I'll take care of everything, Lydia. It's my job to see you back on your feet." Katie hurried from the room, leaving the door ajar in her haste.

Lydia moved off the bed, intending to shut the door and lock it. She realized Katie was really no match for Steven Winters, a man who had rightly earned a ruthless reputation. At the door Lydia's hand gripped its edge as she leaned into it, listening to the exchange between Katie and Steve.

"She doesn't want to see you," Katie said curtly.

"I don't care what she wants. Last night I respected her wishes and left. I'm not going to now. I want to explain why."

"Does it really make any difference why, except

maybe to you? For once, Mr. Winters, consider what Lydia wants and not what you want." Katie's voice was frosty.

With her breath trapped in her lungs, Lydia waited for his reply. She was amazed that she even thought she could keep him out with the flimsy lock on her bedroom door.

"Believe me, it would do you no good to see her."

"Fine," Steve clipped. "But tell her I don't give up that easily."

"I think she's aware of that."

Relieved, Lydia sagged against the door frame. She felt as if she were a criminal having been given a stay of execution.

Lydia loved the sound of the surf. The cool crispness after a rainstorm clung to the early morning air. A heavy dew drenched the nearby plants and glittered like diamonds on the hibiscus blossoms. Nothing was like the tranquility of dawn. She had forgotten how wonderful it was to hear nature awakening to a new day; she was just beginning to realize she had missed a lot with a career that had demanded so much of her.

Tossing back her head, Lydia looked up at the pine trees, their soft willowlike branches swaying gently in the light breeze. Their suppleness was reminiscent of a dancer's body, and Lydia found herself moving her arms in ballet positions to the music of nature.

She felt safe. Steve hadn't called in over a day, and all of yesterday he hadn't appeared on the beach once, not even to jog at dawn. Finally he must have received her message and had probably returned to New York.

Safe but alone. The thought came unbidden into her mind, and all movement of her arms stopped. They fell limply to her sides, the gesture one of defeat.

She wanted to be elated that she didn't ever have to see Steve again, but she wasn't. He had been right. What had happened between them couldn't be wiped away so easily. She had tried enough the last few days with little success.

Maybe after her appointment at the hospital to have her leg cast removed this afternoon she would be able to forget him. Maybe she would be able to concentrate so much on learning to walk that she wouldn't have time to think about the love that might have been hers forever. And maybe she would fly to the moon the next day. Who in the world was she trying to kid?

"Good morning, Lydia. Can we talk?"

The rich timbre of his voice charged the air, distilling the moment in time. One part of her recoiled; the other softened toward the silent plea in his voice.

When she didn't answer, Steve came from behind the log and stood in front of her, his legs braced slightly apart, the breeze ruffling his dark hair. Involuntarily her gaze progressed up the length of him, taking in his lean masculine thighs, his hard, flat stomach, his massive chest, clad in a sleeveless net shirt that revealed muscular arms. Finally she halted her bold inspection at his face, their eyes colliding.

Wearily she replied, "You're certainly persistent. No wonder you got where you are. Okay, say what you have to say, then for God's sake leave me alone. Don't you think I have enough problems to handle without adding you to my list?" Scorn was heavy in her voice.

"You have every right to be feeling what you're

feeling, Lydia. Heaven knows, I didn't want to be the cause of this."

"I'm glad to have your permission to be angry."

Steve shoved his hands into the pockets of his red shorts, staring at the ocean for a moment, then returning his unwavering attention to her. "I think it's more than anger."

"You're damn right, Steve—I mean, Steven. I don't even know what to call you anymore. I feel betrayed, disillusioned. I feel many things toward you." She looked directly into his gray eyes. "Why did you make me love you? I didn't want to fall in love."

"Because you wouldn't take my money."

Lydia gasped, chilled in the warmth of a tropical paradise. "I was right then."

Steve nodded curtly. "Yes, partly. I came to Kauai to make you take the money, so I could get on with my life. You were haunting me and I wasn't any good at Wintercom as long as you and I had unfinished business."

"You came to Hawaii with the idea I was unfinished business, like the European deals," Lydia said, appalled.

Steve tensed, her eyes accusing him. "I wasn't legally responsible for the accident, but still I felt responsible. It was hard for me to come to terms with the fact that I had indirectly caused another person a great deal of pain, physically and emotionally. But when I met you on the beach and began to get to know you, I couldn't tell you who I was. I knew you would reject all offers of help and suddenly the need to help you was even more intense. So I lied and said I was Steve Wilson."

"I can't believe I didn't see through the ruse. But

then I never thought you would go to such lengths to make me take the money."

Steve knelt in front of her, only a foot away. "Don't you see I found myself becoming Steve Wilson, not Steven Winters, corporate executive? I enjoyed my time with you. We laughed, talked, made love."

Lydia glanced away, his nearness suddenly overwhelming. "Please don't remind me of the fool I made of myself."

"Fool?"

She speared him with a lancing look. "Yes! Fool! I fell in love with a figment of my imagination. Steve Wilson doesn't exist then or now. So you don't need to worry about someone asking for a commitment."

Steve started to take her hands in his, but Lydia shrank back, blindly fumbling for her crutches. She had to get away from him. Her fingers clamped around the wood and she hurriedly positioned her crutches in front of her to stand. If she didn't escape soon she would make a further fool of herself and cry for what might have been.

As quickly as possible she headed for her house, the tears that had been threatening, now streaming down her face. The bleak despair in Steve's eyes when she had flinched away from him haunted her.

Inside, Lydia sank onto the couch, squeezing her eyes shut.

She had fallen in love with Steve Wilson and she didn't know the man who called himself Steven Winters. She buried her face in her hands, wondering what was going to become of them. One part of her hated him, but the other still loved the man who had hit her.

"Do you want something to eat before we go to the hospital?" Katie asked from the doorway leading into the kitchen.

Lydia scrubbed the tears from her face, resolving to take one crisis at a time. The first thing she had to do was have her cast removed, then she had to concentrate on learning to walk. After that she would sort through the emotional traumas.

"No, I don't think I could eat a thing. My stomach is tied up in knots as it is. I'm going to call Jason, so go ahead and eat."

"Fine. I'll be ready to leave in thirty minutes."

Katie hadn't said anything about her red eyes, but Lydia knew she was worried. In fact, Katie had been very concerned about her for the past few days. The day before Katie had even gotten angry at her because she was pushing herself too hard with her therapy.

Lydia reached for the phone and placed her call through to Jason. "How's everything going there?"

"Better this past week. I was going to call you later to tell you Maggie and I will be in Kauai in five days. She's saying a few words now, Sis. I grant you, not much, but it is a start."

"Oh, Jason, I'm glad to hear that. I was hoping you two would be able to come soon."

"Do I detect boredom?" Jason asked with a laugh.

No, an urgent need for company, Lydia silently answered, then aloud said, "I just want to see my two favorite people. I'll see you in five days."

Her left leg was freed of its plaster confines, but all that Lydia could think about was the time that Steve had been with her when they had taken off her arm cast. He had stood by her, his gentle support apparent in their clasped hands, the tender look in his eyes. She wished she had him now; she ached for him to be by her side. She wanted him to share in her happiness; she wanted them to celebrate like before. She wanted a lot.

Still using the crutches, Lydia walked from the hospital toward the car with Katie. There would be no quaint little restaurant. There would be no lovemaking afterward. There would be nothing. After this morning she wouldn't be surprised if Steve was gone from the house next door.

On the silent ride back to the beach house, Lydia tried to think of something to say to Katie, but her thoughts revolved around Steve and she couldn't discuss him with anyone. Her feelings were so confused that it would be extremely hard to place them into words.

A cooler sat at the sliding glass door, blocking the entrance into the house. Puzzled, Katie bent and lifted the top. She laughed and held up the box that had been inside the cooler. Inside the box was a huge chocolate bar that formed the words "I'm sorry. I was the fool." Suddenly the grave situation was lightened. Lydia smiled for the first time in days.

"That's an unusual apology," Katie said as she opened the door, pushing the cooler aside so Lydia could enter the house.

"I think I'm just beginning to realize how unusual a man Steven Winters is."

Lydia didn't waste any time starting her therapy session. She didn't want to use the crutches much longer and so she worked hard, strengthening the unused muscles of her leg and running through one strenuous exercise after another. Soon she would be able to bear the weight and use a cane.

That evening after dinner, Lydia placed a classical record on the stereo and sat in the middle of the living room floor. She ran through some stretch exercises to the music, a limited version of what she used to do every day when she was dancing. By the time she had completed some of the dance movements, she felt alive, in tune with her body for the first time since the accident. There was a bad pain in her left leg, but she had a goal in mind that made it tolerable.

Lydia went to bed early and slept hard, waking at dawn, as usual. She quickly dressed in a cotton shirt and shorts and headed for the beach. Apprehensive, she sat down on the log and waited, praying that Steven hadn't gone back to New York.

There had been no lights on the night before at his house, so when an hour had passed, Lydia feared the worse. Steven was gone and she hadn't given them a chance.

Struggling to her feet, she started toward the house when suddenly she came to an abrupt halt. Through the bushes she saw his house and decided to leave the path and make her way toward it.

She was negotiating the stairs that led to his redwood deck when the sliding glass door banged open. A harried-looking Steven rushed from the house, only to stop on the top step when he saw her, a stunned expression on his face.

"Lydia! What are you doing here?"

She never thought she would see Steven so openly surprised. He stood paralyzed on his deck, half dressed with his shirt still clutched in his hand.

Lydia looked from his face to his shirt that dangled at his side. Her mouth twitched with silent laughter. "Going somewhere?" She arched a brow as he often did.

Steven shook his head slightly as though to clear it, then gazed down at his shirt. Quickly he slipped it over his head. When his head emerged from the shirt, he appeared amused.

"I overslept," he explained as he followed the progression of Lydia's regard to his bare feet. "I thought I might have missed you."

"And I thought you had gone back to New York."

"Would that have bothered you?"

Her gaze shot instantly to his face, his eyes pleading for her honesty. "Yes."

"Will you come inside for some coffee?"

She nodded.

Stepping to the side, Steven allowed her to pass him. He opened the door but let her walk inside on her own.

Seated at the kitchen table, Lydia watched as he fixed a pot of coffee. She took pleasure in following his movements about the room, as if this had been going on for years.

The odor of brewing coffee saturated the air as Steven folded his long length into the chair opposite her at the table. "I'm almost afraid to ask why you're here. I think I'm going to lean back and enjoy the sight of you for a few more minutes." His expression was serious as he relaxed back in the chair with his arms crossed, his eyes roving over her features in admiration.

Lydia blushed, raising her hand in protest. "Steven, you're making me nervous. Stop that!"

"Do you want me to look at something else? I suppose I could watch the coffeepot. But I must say, that wouldn't be nearly as interesting as you."

"I want to talk and I can't when you're looking that way at me." She stifled a laugh. It was difficult not to feel joyous when Steven was staring at her with desire. All the suppressed feelings about him were quickly rekindled.

"I meant what I sent you yesterday, every delicious word."

"I think we've both been more confused than foolish. I've never met anyone quite like you."

"Lydia, I didn't start out wanting to lie to you about who I was. But when I sensed so strongly that you would have had nothing to do with me as Steven Winters, I lied. It was so important to me that you accept my help. It was easier to try to help you financially, but you rejected that so absolutely that I had to do something. I started out only intending to stay a week, but that quickly became two, then three." His voice was rough and low, faintly gritty with emotions.

"Steven, why didn't you go back to New York yesterday after we talked on the beach? I didn't give you much encouragement."

"I tried to fly out last night. I was at the airport about to board my plane when, suddenly, I couldn't bring myself to get on it. I couldn't leave without trying one more time with you, Lydia." He reached out and covered her hand with his, his smile wistful, tentative. "I'm not sure what's happening to me. Yesterday at the airport I didn't feel like Steven Winters. I was Steve Wilson. And as Steve Wilson, I had no reason to return to work," he said with an intently inquiring look. "Does that make any sense to you?"

"I think so."

"Good." He flashed her a quick smile. "Then explain it to me."

His thumb began an absorbing study of her hand, a disturbing sensuality in his touch that Lydia had tried to deny. He continued his sensual survey at her wrist, her pulse stimulated to a fast pace.

"You aren't the same man as before. Steven Winters came to Hawaii, but once you assumed Steve Wilson's name, I think things started happening to you. Do I make sense?"

His fingers wrapped themselves tightly about her hand. "Oh, Lydia, there's so much changing inside of me. I think before I came here, I was dissatisfied with the way my life was going. Your accident was the catalyst for me to start doing something about it. But I am confused and scared as hell. I don't know the man I'm becoming." The wry line of his mouth communicated his unease. Humor, directed at himself, flared in his eyes.

Lydia placed her other hand over their clasped ones. "I know what you're going through. I'm no longer Lydia Masters, prima ballerina, but Lydia Masters, a woman searching for a new direction in her life."

When she had said prima ballerina, Steven had grown taut, his eyes clouding with sorrow. "I did that to you."

"No, you didn't. I've finally realized it was all my fault. I can't even blame you partially. You were convenient, Steven, for me to direct my anger at. I had a fleeting, temporary direction to my life in hating you."

His eyes locked with hers. "Do you hate me now?"

"No." She paused, running her tongue over her dry lips. "But like you, I believe we both need some time to evaluate what's happened to us. I want to discover who Steven Winters really is. I fell in love with Steve Wilson and he doesn't exist."

"Not totally. I want that time with you, too, because for the first time in my life I really care what another person thinks about me. I want us to begin again as Steven Winters and Lydia Masters, two people searching for something. No more lies between us."

"I would like that. Can you stay a while longer?"

"For once I'll make time for myself. I don't want to walk away without knowing if there's a future for us. You see, Steve Wilson wasn't a loner. He needed you. The only thing I lied about was my name, not my feelings."

His gentle tone made her realize she was still very much in love with Steve Wilson. Were they really two distinct people or the same man?

"Now, how about that cup of coffee I promised you?" Steven asked, releasing her hand and rising.

"Lots of cream and sugar."

He laughed, the sound wonderful to Lydia. "One sweetened milk flavored with coffee coming up."

After filling their mugs, Steven sat back down but this time next to Lydia. "I wish I had been with you yesterday when you had your cast removed. How are things coming along?"

"Better than I expected. I have a reason to be

walking quickly—I want you to see me without my casts and standing on my own two feet."

He sipped his coffee, his eyes never letting go of hers. "Let's go back to that restaurant tonight. We'll call it our first real date."

"And what do you call the first time?"

"That was under false pretenses. This won't be." He extended his hand. "Friends?"

"More than friends."

She shook his hand, looking deeply into his eyes. Slowly raising her hand to his mouth, he teased the palm of her hand with the tip of his tongue.

"Yes, much more," he murmured.

Chapter Twelve

The strong wind created by the helicopter whipped Lydia's hair away from her face. She leaned heavily upon her walking cane as she made her way toward the aircraft. This was her first day using her cane and she felt so free, now that her crutches were discarded.

Steven assisted her into the helicopter, then climbed in next to her. He had planned this outing to a secluded beach that could only be reached by helicopter or boat. This was their time to be alone before Jason and Maggie arrived later that day.

Lydia settled back into her seat and completely relaxed as the chopper took off from the Princeville Airport. The past four days spent in Steven's company had been exciting, learning about each other, an intimate relationship developing between them.

There were times she felt as if she floated through each day with Steven, even though she was working hard at her therapy. Katie had left for Honolulu, her job completed. Now it would only take time for Lydia to walk without the cane and slight limp.

Steven laid his hand on her knee, smiling at her with a warmth that radiated from his eyes. The dimples in his cheeks were deep with his contentment. Lydia responded to his smile with her own, placing her hand over his.

She now knew she loved Steven Winters. The man she had known the past days was the same gentle, kind, sensitive man as Steve Wilson. If Steven Winters had earned the title of lone wolf, she hadn't seen any of that. During the long hours they had spent together, he had told her everything about himself, his troubling relationship with his brother, his intense drive to work, his childhood, and his love for music that matched hers. She had learned of his overwhelming disappointment at having to give up his dream of becoming a classical guitarist, of how he had thrown himself into making Wintercom a thriving corporation as a way of trying to forget what he couldn't have.

Her hand tightened about his. The helicopter banked to the left and Steven pointed out the side window at the Waimea Canyon below. She no longer looked upon the barren canyon as her future life—not if she could share it with Steven.

They flew along the rim of the canyon toward the Na Pali Coast, the view from the helicopter more breathtaking than from the lookouts.

Twenty minutes later they landed on a deserted beach, a cove surrounded by cliffs and the shimmering ocean with the sun glinting off its surface. Steven hopped out of the chopper, then helped Lydia down before grabbing for the picnic basket and blanket.

"I'll pick you two up at three," the pilot said before taking off.

Lydia held her sun hat on her head until the wind from the helicopter died down and only the soft ocean breeze caressed her face. Steven slid his arm about her waist and she leaned into him, savoring the quiet, the peace of being totally alone with Steven.

"I'm glad you thought of this, Steven." Lydia nestled closer to him.

"I'm just sorry I didn't think of this sooner. This is beautiful." He waved his arm in a wide arc, his gesture encompassing all of the primitive beauty about them.

She laughed lightly. "I might have had a little problem with negotiating this beach in a cast or on crutches."

He turned toward her, cupping her chin and tilting it up toward his face. "We would have managed," he murmured, slowly lowering his mouth toward hers.

Their lips met in a gentle whisper, his hand slipping down her neck in a languid motion. His mouth stirred upon hers, and the kiss evolved into a elemental mating. Its forcefulness parted her lips and his tongue delved within, inspecting the soft interior with bold caresses.

Embracing her, her cane dropping to the sand, Steven buried his face in the loose waves of her hair. "We only have a few hours until the pilot comes back." His voice was rugged. "Why couldn't it have been a few days?"

Thrilling at the passionate words, Lydia hugged

Steven tightly to her. She didn't think she would ever take for granted the pleasure of being able to hold him, both her arms enveloping him. She breathed in the male odor of him that blended with the salty scent of the ocean.

They stood on the beach for a long time, their arms entwined about each other, until Steven drew back slightly and smiled crookedly down at her. "Are you hungry? I have a feeling if we don't eat now we won't at all."

She touched his cheek, the love she felt glowing in her eyes. "Yes, which is strange. Whenever I'm nervous, I don't eat."

His brow wrinkled in puzzlement. "What are you nervous about? Surely not being here . . ." His voice trailed off into silence, then he asked, "Is it Jason and Maggie's visit that has you worried?"

"Yes. I'm not sure how Maggie is going to receive me. I'm not sure how she's going to react to being so far away from home, even though I feel that home held a lot of horrible memories for her. She's still so unstable."

"You'll know the right thing to do when you see her. You seem to have a knack for that. I think I could take a few lessons from you." Steven cradled her to him as they walked to the picnic basket.

"You're worried about Eric, aren't you? Have you heard any more from him?"

"No and I don't know if that's a good sign. Tyler tells me Eric is showing up for work and the expansion plans are progressing, but still . . ." Steven shook his head, combing his fingers through his wind-tousled hair.

Steven wore dark sunglasses, but Lydia didn't have to see his eyes to know of his concern. "But still you have a feeling something is wrong."

"I can't shake the feeling. I tried calling him several times the last few days. There hasn't been an answer at home and I hate bothering him at work about our personal differences." Steven bent and spread a blanket out on the beach.

Lydia stretched out on the cover and opened the basket. "Maybe you should if it's bothering you that much."

"I guess I should at least inquire about how the project is coming along. I should have pressed him about the reason he needed that twenty-five thousand dollars, but at the time I was tired of being used by my brother and I wasn't thinking straight."

Steven had discussed the scene in which Eric had tried to blackmail him, and Lydia was worried, too. If Eric did anything rash, Steven would have a hard time forgiving himself. He might not always show it to the world, but Steven had deep feelings for the people he cared about, his family and his co-workers.

"Call him tonight when we get back and if you don't reach your brother, then try tomorrow at work." Lydia handed Steven the bottle of chilled white wine for him to open while she prepared their plates with cold fried chicken, various sliced fruits, and freshly baked bread.

"I guess I've been trying to avoid talking with Eric because I hate to spoil the contented mood I've been in lately. We always end up arguing. I never say the right thing to him even though I might have good intentions. You and Jason get along well. How do you do it?"

"Well, for starters, we aren't competing in the same business. Jason has a hard time doing a simple dance step, let alone something like ballet. And I"—Lydia rolled her eyes heavenward—"can't carry a tune. People flee when they hear me sing."

His deep laughter ricocheted off the cliffs. "Surely you aren't that bad."

"Then I'll just have to give you a demonstration someday when you're not imprisoned by these cliffs. I wouldn't want to be accused of torturing you."

The light bantering mood prevailed throughout their lunch as Lydia described some of the antics she and Jason used to pull as children.

"We drove our parents crazy. And to this day Mom and Dad still won't let Jason or me forget some of the things we did to terrorize the neighborhood."

"Where are you from?"

"Louisville. My parents still live there, retired school teachers."

"Do you ever get to see them much?" Steven refilled their wine glasses, emptying the bottle.

"Not nearly enough for them and I must say for myself, too. Actually even with Jason's busy road schedule, he's managed to get home more than I have."

"Why didn't you go home after the accident?"

Staring into her wine, Lydia ran her finger around the top of her glass, then lifted her gaze to meet the dark mask of Steven's sunglasses. "I had to do this alone—or at least I thought I had to. But when you showed up, I knew I needed to share the struggle with someone. You made me realize I shouldn't shut myself away from the people who care about me."

Steven tossed back his head and drained the last of his wine. "I think that's what I've been doing all my life. I live a short drive from my mother's house on Long Island and I bet I don't see her much more than you have seen your parents, who live hundreds of miles away."

"You know it's easy to get wrapped up in your work, thinking the other will always be there later when you've completed the job you're working on. But the trouble with that is that you usually move on to something else. Your life becomes a succession of tasks."

"Put in those words, that's not a very appealing life."

"It's a very limited life."

Steven relaxed back on an elbow, his eyes still concealed behind the sunglasses, but Lydia could feel his intense regard. He reached across the expanse of blanket and ran his finger along her jawline, the touch so soft it felt like the wings of a hummingbird brushing against her face. It induced a weak giddiness within Lydia, far more potent than the white wine.

She couldn't resist the urge any longer. Lifting his sunglasses from his nose, she was struck by the overpowering look of desire within the gray depths. Their glow matched the diamond-shimmering ocean behind Lydia.

Steven seized her hand, the sunglasses falling to the blanket. Bringing her hand to his mouth, he nibbled playfully on each fingertip. "Mmm, salty." He looked up, amusement dancing in his eyes. "I always had a thing about salt."

"Like my chocolate fetish. I ate your apology in two

days." He was taking her breath away with his sensual attack on her senses. Her hand felt on fire, the hot moistness of his tongue making lazy circles in her palm.

"My craving for salt definitely hasn't been satisfied. Maybe I should taste more of you."

He gently shoved her back onto the blanket and pinned her to the sand with his body, his face only inches from hers. Grazing her lips with his once then twice, he laughed, a deliciously delightful sound caused by the pure joy of the moment.

"You are so beautiful, my darling. I wish we never had to leave this place."

"Then let's don't. We could run away."

A sobering expression canceled out the gleam of humor in Steven's eyes. For a moment staring down at her, he was suspended above her by stiff arms. Then with an ardent savagery, he crushed his mouth down onto hers, the grinding pressure demanding, almost desperate. Her hands dug into his shoulders and she clung to him.

Pulling back, Steven rolled off Lydia, his chest rising and falling rapidly as he dragged the tropical-scented air into his lungs. "Lydia, I wish I could stay here, but I have to return to New York soon."

Everything seemed to stop moving, the world at a standstill, her world. She had known the time would come when Steven would have to say those words. She had thought she was prepared. She wasn't.

"When?" She couldn't stop her voice from quavering.

Lydia sat up, her legs drawn against her chest, her arms curled about them. She stared unseeingly at the waves that relentlessly hammered at the shoreline. No matter what, she wasn't going to make this hard for Steven. She had promised him no strings attached. But for the life of her she didn't know how she was going to pull it off. Closing her eyes against the threatening tears, she fortified herself with several deep breaths.

"In three or four days. I've been away too long. I need to be there first thing Monday morning."

She didn't reply. What could she say?

"Lydia?" His hand stroked the length of her spine.

She twisted about and said in as steady a voice as possible, "Then we have a few more days and we'll make the most of them. Hold me, Steven. Make love to me now and every day until you have to leave."

"If I had my way, I would lock you up in my bedroom and we wouldn't come out for the next four days." Steven drew her down upon him, his arms winding about her to hold her close to him.

For a long time he just held her, his hand brushing down her long brown hair, as they both allowed this special moment to pass only to be treasured during those times when they would be apart.

Then Steven pulled her up to settle her mouth upon his, rolling her over onto her back. While he deepened the kiss, his hand slowly traveled under her T-shirt to fill it with the fullness of her breast. With leisurely thoroughness his tongue investigated her mouth; his hand explored her breasts, eliciting each nipple to hard peaks. While his tongue pushed deep into the cavity of her mouth, his hand journeyed lower until it discovered the waistband of her shorts. While his mouth seared a path to her earlobe, teasing the hypersensitive skin with the tip of his tongue, his hand slipped between her flat stomach and waistband and pushed the material down.

They didn't have all the time in the world, but Steven made love to her as if there were no tomorrow. He had told her once he couldn't promise her tomorrow, but she wanted all those tomorrows.

His roughened hands searched her hidden places that aroused her beyond coherence, his mouth following suit. A bond of magic held them bound together as the exquisite tension Steven had painstakingly built within her crested and crashed against the shore where only lovers played.

When he moved off her minutes later, Lydia didn't want to sever that bond. She pressed her length along his, toying with the hair on his chest, her fingers roaming over him in an almost thoughtful motion. She reached a decision as she watched a bird soar, then swoop down to land on a tree branch on the side of the cliff.

"I love you, Steven Winters. You aren't two men but one. I just suspect you've kept the other hidden because of the demands that have been placed on you."

Steven hugged her tightly to him. "In the state of mind I've been in lately, I've been afraid to make any kind of commitment. It could be temporary and I don't want to ever hurt you any more than I have. I've done enough of that to last a lifetime." He paused, clearing his throat. "I know I don't have a right to ask for time, but I know the type of man I've been over the last seventeen years. I'm not sure I can change. I'm not sure of a lot of things. And that's what's so damn frustrating."

"Time is something I have a lot of." Lydia sat up and began dressing. "I know this was the wrong time in our lives to have met, but there are some things we have no control over." She turned around and faced Steven, who still lay on the blanket, his crossed arms cushioning his head. "I didn't want you to go back to New York and not know how I feel. I want you to know that I don't hold any part of that accident your fault. You are a free man, debt paid in full if not more, Steven Winters. What you have given me these past weeks is more than most people ever would have, and it has meant more to me than any amount of money you could have paid me. You have helped me see myself as a woman, not a dancer. Without your guidance I'm not sure I would have ever discovered it. Thank you." Tracing the outline of his mouth, she stamped the image of Steven into her mind forever. She was suddenly afraid those tomorrows would never be hers.

Steven kissed the palm of her hand, then tugged her gently down upon him. "But what if your love is really only gratitude, Lydia? I was there for you when you needed someone very much. Perhaps someone else could have fulfilled that for you just as well."

"I don't think what I feel for you is gratitude, but the things you did are all bound up in the reasons I fell in love with you in the first place. You can't separate them."

"Then you don't know for sure."

Lydia rubbed her mouth back and forth across his. "I never stopped and thought about it."

He captured her face within his hands and held her away. "Then maybe you should, Lydia."

The sound of a helicopter in the distance brought Steven to his feet and he quickly dressed while Lydia gathered up the remains of their lunch and the blanket. Nothing was settled between them, but she knew in her heart what she felt for Steven wasn't gratitude. There was wisdom, though, in waiting, because she still had a very important decision to make. What to do for the rest of her life? Until she knew that answer her life was still suspended in limbo.

Steven clasped Lydia's hand tightly as she watched the plane land. Lines of worry were etched into her face as she stood next to Steven, feeling slightly better with his silent strength beside her.

"Everything is going to be all right," he murmured into her ear, placing a light kiss upon it.

She smiled up at him, a faint lifting of the corners of her mouth. "I hope so. Maggie used to be such a happy child, always laughing and playing with the neighborhood kids."

"She's been in therapy and your brother said there's been progress," Steven pointed out as the passengers began to disembark.

When she saw Jason and Maggie walking toward her, she removed her hand from Steven's and made her way toward her brother and niece. Jason's eyes were alight with relief as he neared Lydia.

"Oh, Sis, you look wonderful. This warm, tropical air has done wonders for you." He kissed her and when he pulled away, he glanced beyond Lydia to Steven. "Is that Steve, the guy who lives next door?"

Lydia hadn't told her brother that Steve Wilson was really Steven Winters. It wasn't something she felt she could explain on the phone. She nodded, then turned her attention to her niece, who stood slightly behind Jason.

"Hello, Maggie."

The young girl looked up at her with round, sad eyes. She made no attempt to say anything nor to accept Lydia's extended hand, but she did smile faintly at her aunt.

"It's been an extremely long, taxing trip, Lydia. I think we both need some rest and relaxation."

"Yes, of course," Lydia murmured, wanting so much to hug her niece and tell her everything would be all right. But Maggie wasn't ready for it.

Steven approached them and said, "I'm Steven Winters. If you give me your claim checks, I'll see about your luggage."

Shock registered on Jason's face. Trancelike he handed Steven the tickets. When Steven had disappeared, Jason asked, "That couldn't be the man who hit you, could it?"

"Yes."

"Lydia, I thought—"

"I'll explain later after we've gotten you two settled in at the house."

After Steven had located Jason's two pieces of luggage, they headed for Steven's sedan, where Jason and Maggie sat in the back while Lydia was in the front, very aware of Jason's puzzled expression as he looked from her to Steven. On the drive toward the north shore Lydia tried to bring Maggie out, but her niece didn't say anything the whole trip. After a while Lydia decided that she was pushing too hard and fell silent. Steven glanced sideways at her and smiled his reassurances that everything would be all right. He took her hand and held it clasped between them on the seat most of the way to the beach house.

Inside the house, Steven placed the suitcases in the

bedroom across from Lydia's, then turned to her. "I need to use your phone. I think I'd better try to reach Eric before it gets too late in New York."

"One of the phone extensions is in my room. Use that one. I'm going to fix Maggie a snack and then put her to bed."

Steven dropped a light kiss on her forehead, then walked into her bedroom, quietly closing the door. Even though his actions were casual, Lydia could tell he was anxious about talking with his brother. Sighing deeply, she made her way to the kitchen while Jason settled his daughter in the third bedroom. As Lydia prepared a ham sandwich and a glass of milk for Maggie, her thoughts were with Steven. She halfway hoped he didn't get in touch with his brother; every time they talked there was a confrontation. She wanted this time left to her to be free of strife, but she guessed with Jason and Maggie here now that would be impossible.

Lydia had carried the plate with the sandwich and glass on it to Maggie's bedroom and had tactfully withdrawn to allow her niece some time alone with Jason. Her leg throbbed from standing too long on it and she limped toward the living room. She was propping her foot up when Steven came into the room, a frown slashing his rugged features.

"Did you get in touch with Eric?"

"No. And Tyler isn't home either. I think I'm going to take your suggestion and call first thing tomorrow morning. I'll feel better when I hear everything is okay." Steven eased his body onto the couch next to Lydia and slipped his arm about her shoulder, absently stroking her.

"Well, from what you've told me about Eric, it's not unusual that he's out."

"But my male intuition tells me all is not well." His glance flicked toward her leg. "Is it hurting?"

"A little, but that's not unusual. I've been on it too much today."

"We probably overdid it, especially with your brother arriving." His fingers began to massage her shoulders and neck as he continued, "You hadn't told him who I was."

"Jason knew about Steve Wilson, not Steven Winters."

He chuckled. "I imagine that would be difficult to explain."

She nodded, closing her eyes to the sweet rapture of his hands. Swaying back against him, she succumbed to the intimacy of the moment.

"I think Maggie is out like a light," Jason said as he entered the living room, the deep lines of exhaustion about his eyes more evident than earlier when he had gotten off the plane.

Steven stopped the delicious massage and fitted Lydia securely within the curve of his arm. His body heat made her feverish with desire.

"May I get you two a drink? That wasn't an easy plane ride with Maggie." Jason walked to the bar and poured himself a straight whiskey.

"I'll take a whiskey and soda and—"

"I'll have a glass of white wine," Lydia completed the order.

After Jason had placed the drinks in Lydia's and Steven's hands and had collapsed in the lounge chair across from them, he said what had obviously been on his mind since he and Steven had met. "You're the man who was driving the car." It was a question as much as a statement.

"Yes."

"But she told me you were Steve Wilson." Suspicion edged Jason's words.

"I was, at first."

Lydia laughed at her brother who was scowling at Steven. It had reminded her that older brothers were really overprotective. "Jason, everything is fine, so you can stop that scowling of yours."

"But, Lydia, in the hospital . . ." His words died on his lips as he looked at the apparent intimacy between Lydia and Steven.

"In the hospital I was in shock, bitter and very angry at the fates. I'm not saying I'm completely over those feelings, but I am coming to terms with the changes." She slid a glance toward Steven, burrowing even deeper into the crook of his arm. "Mainly because I met a man who helped me through the rough times when I thought I could stand alone and do it all by myself. He didn't take no for an answer but instead was persistent." Lydia explained how she had met Steve Wilson, who had later turned out to be Steven Winters.

"Wow, that's some story." Jason downed his drink, then walked to the bar to refill his glass. "Want any more?"

Lydia shook her head while Steven answered no.

"I guess I should thank you," Jason said, sitting back down in the lounge chair, "but I've been so used to cursing the day you were born it might take some getting used to. Though I am happy to see you smiling, Lydia. That's worth a hell of a lot to me."

The weary defeat in Jason's voice prompted Lydia to ask, "How are things going with Maggie?"

"I thought, until this trip, better. But she didn't say one word the whole time she was on the plane. She had been beginning to talk a little and now I'm afraid we're back to square one. I guess this trip was a mistake after all. But since I've sold the house, I thought this would be a good transition before we moved into our new home."

"Give her time to adjust. Take it from an expert on changes, she needs the time. A lot has happened to Maggie in the last year." Lydia jumped slightly at the sound of the phone ringing, then she leaned sideways and picked it up.

"Is Steven Winters there?" a deep baritone voice asked.

"Yes, just a minute." She handed the receiver to Steven.

The silence in the room was punctuated with a few curt words from Steven, then the slamming of the receiver down onto its cradle. The lean planes of his face hardened into a thunderous expression, his body completely tense.

"I have to leave, Lydia." He slid his arm from around her shoulders and stood. "That was Tyler on the phone and there's a grave problem at Wintercom that needs my immediate attention."

"I'll go with you to help you pack," Lydia replied, trying to keep her alarm at bay. When he had been talking with Tyler on the phone, she had watched him transform into the Steven Winters who ran a large corporation and had to make difficult decisions every day that often involved hundreds of people and thousands of dollars. She was very frightened. Steven was slipping away from her faster than she had thought.

Together in silence, they walked to Steven's house, where he immediately headed for his bedroom to throw his clothes into a suitcase. Lydia sat on his bed, trying to bring some kind of order to the chaos. It was useless because he continued to toss more clothes into the suitcase before she could fold the last piece.

"Steven, what's the problem?"

He halted clearing out his dresser and pivoted toward her. "Someone's embezzled a large sum of Wintercom's money. I'm being sabotaged from within. This weekend I have to find out who did it."

"Do you have any ideas who did it?"

The bright light that usually sparkled in his eyes died completely as he muttered, "Yes, Eric."

"Oh, no, Steven!"

"The facts add up. He needed money for some unknown reason and he had access to the books as well as the know-how. He may not realize it, but I do know how smart my little brother is. He's kept it hidden, but I know."

"What are you going to do?"

"Follow through on my threat. Kick him out of the company. I can't keep spoon-feeding him or constantly keep an eye on his every move. I just pray to God it isn't him. It would kill Mother."

Beneath the hard exterior, Lydia could sense his anguish. It would not only kill Steven's mother but him as well.

She wanted to go to him and hold him tightly to her but his look forbade it. Instead, she silently watched him finish his packing and click the suitcase shut. The sound was so final that Lydia shuddered.

They made their way toward the front door where Lydia glanced back once more at the house she had grown to feel was theirs. Her heartbeat decreased to a slow throb as Steven closed the door behind them.

After stowing his luggage in the front seat, he turned toward her, his arms stiff at his sides. He opened his mouth to speak, then closed it. Lydia found herself holding her breath.

"Oh, God, Lydia, I wish I could tell you that I love you. I think I do, but the plain truth of the matter is I'm not sure. I know what my life was like back in New York and I don't know if I've changed enough to make any difference. I do know the old me avoids commitments for a good reason. I—"

Lydia silenced his words with the tips of her fingers. "I believe it will do us both some good to be apart and to think." She tried to smile, but her lips wouldn't respond to the signal from her brain. "But right now, you have a plane to catch and a problem to handle. I pray Eric isn't the one. I know how much that would hurt you. My thoughts go with you." Her throat constricted, and the last sentence barely made it past her lips. She had a horrible feeling that this was the last time she would see Steven.

He took her head within his large hands and brought his mouth down upon hers with a melting gentleness that shook her to her very core. She wanted to turn her back on Jason and Maggie and beg Steven to take her with him. But at the same time, she knew she would only be in his way. He needed room to solve not only his problem with Wintercom but to sort out his confusion and the changes that had recently taken place.

His arms became a tight ring about her, pressing her into his body until she felt every sinewy plane. The fierceness of his embrace robbed her of her breath and yet she was reluctant to sever the closeness.

Steven buried his face into her hair and whispered hoarsely, "Don't forget what I told you. You're very special." With a quick squeeze that nearly crushed her bones, he stepped away. "I'll call."

Then he strode to his car and climbed in behind the wheel. The engine roared to life, disturbing the quiet night.

The trembling began in her hands as she lifted one to wave good-bye, but rapidly it spread throughout her body. With tears cascading down her face, she watched the car disappear from view and couldn't rid herself of the feeling that her life would never be the same. Part of her was in that car she could no longer see.

Chapter Thirteen

$\mathcal{T}$he music was loud and her movements were limited, but at least she was dancing, even if she wasn't bearing much weight on her left ankle.

Lydia bent and swayed with the sensuous rhythm that vividly brought to mind pictures of her and Steven making love. She lost herself in the sounds as she often had done while performing. The soft melody filled her soul.

The tempo increased and built to its finish. Lydia sagged down onto the floor, breathing deeply. Pushing from her thoughts the nagging ache in her ankle, she lifted her head and found Maggie staring at her from the doorway into the living room. A spark of interest was evident in her niece's wide, sad eyes, and Lydia decided to try something with Maggie.

She motioned for her niece to enter the room while she flipped the record over to its other side. Then Lydia sat cross-legged on the floor and moved her upper body slowly to the beat of the music. Her arms were a graceful extension that floated in the air, then fluttered like a bird's wings.

Maggie stood for a moment, watching, then suddenly she sat on the floor next to Lydia and tried to imitate her arm movements. As the rhythm of the music became faster, Maggie no longer looked to Lydia but improvised instead. Maggie's arms slashed through the air, her head thrown back. The music ended and Maggie was curled in a ball, a frenzy of spent energy.

For a long time stunned, Lydia sat quietly beside her niece. Maggie had a lot of anger deep inside of her that she hadn't expressed since her mother's death, not even in therapy.

"Maggie?" Lydia touched her niece tentatively on the shoulder.

Maggie straightened, looked at Lydia, then suddenly wrapped her thin arms about Lydia's neck, hugging her tightly. That was the first time her niece had shown any intense emotions toward her since her mother's accident.

When Jason came into the living room, he halted in mid-stride and stared at his daughter and sister. Lydia glanced up and smiled. Her brother looked so tired, a troubled expression always just under the surface. Jason and Maggie had been on Kauai three days and Maggie hadn't even wanted to go to the beach. Every morning he would come into the room and try to persuade Maggie to go out with him. Every morning she would shake her head.

"Well, I don't know about you two, but it's a beautiful day and the beach is just out there waiting for us," Jason said with a forced cheerfulness that tore at Lydia's heart.

"You know I love the sun," Lydia whispered against the top of Maggie's head.

Her niece still held her tightly, but slowly Maggie unwound her arms and stared up into Lydia's face. "Your leg looks funny, Aunt Lydia."

Lydia hid her surprise behind a wide smile as she combed Maggie's hair back from her face. "I need to get it tan; someone will have to tell me when to turn over so that I tan evenly. Will you come to the beach, too?"

Maggie nodded.

"Let's get ready, then." Jason helped Lydia to her feet while Maggie bounced up and hurried toward her bedroom. "What happened, Lydia?"

With a puzzled expression on her face, Lydia watched Maggie go into her bedroom. "I'm not sure, Jason. But tomorrow when I'm doing my dance exercises, I'm going to try and persuade Maggie to work with me." Turning to her brother, she asked, "Has the therapist ever talked to you about Maggie's anger?"

"Anger? Well, some. But Maggie is just lonely. She misses her mother. We both do."

"Jason, she's more than lonely. I think she's a very angry little girl."

"Why?" Jason asked incredulously.

"Because you were on the road a lot and Maggie looked to Diana for everything. Then suddenly Maggie's world was turned upside down when her mother died. I know what it's like, Jason."

"But you aren't angry anymore."

"No, but it took time and I had someone special to

help me through the tough times." Lydia started to walk toward her bedroom to dress for the beach.

"Have you heard from Steven since he left for New York?"

At the doorway Lydia glanced back. "No, but it's only been three days."

Three long, miserable days without Steven, Lydia added silently as she went to her bedroom. She had kept telling herself over and over that he had a crisis on his hands and that he would call when he could. But the doubts were still there.

With a tightly controlled movement, Steven replaced the receiver. When he had finally been able to grab a few minutes to call Lydia, she hadn't been at her beach house. He was beginning to wonder if he was really kidding himself to even think they had a chance. When he had arrived back in New York three days before, he had immediately immersed himself into the problem at hand and as usual he didn't have time for anything else. No one knew he was even back except Tyler.

Steven sagged back in his desk chair, scanning his office almost absently. Then his gaze fastened on the ledgers before him. The person who had embezzled was damn good, that was for sure. He had a good hunch who was responsible, but until he had proof, he wouldn't say anything. He couldn't say anything. If it was the person he thought, it was still hard for him to believe it. But it was beginning to look as if one of his competitors had paid for this man's services in messing up the French deal that backfired. So now the man was looking for another way to get rich fast.

Steven swung his chair around to stare out the large

window behind his desk. The lights of Manhattan greeted him, shimmering in the darkness. It was Sunday evening when everyone else was home with his family, but he was working as usual. Maybe the old pattern was just too hard for him to change. It hadn't taken him five minutes to fall back into the routine and tonight he wasn't even sure if he would make it home to sleep in his own bed. He wanted this problem settled by Monday morning.

With a heavy sigh Steven whirled his chair back around and leaned forward, his elbows resting on the desk, to examine the books again. Hour after hour he poured over the ledgers and the evidence that Tyler had been able to gather, and finally near dawn he knew the answer with no doubt and absolute proof.

Damn! He was tired of all this, exhausted in both body and mind. Rubbing his hands over his face, he shoved his fingers through his already tousled hair, then stood to stretch his aching muscles. He rolled his back and kneaded the taut cords of his neck. The action brought Lydia to mind. He needed her right now, but it was in the middle of the night in Hawaii. Even though, it was difficult for him to resist the strong urge to call her just to hear her voice.

After he had shaved and changed into a freshly pressed suit, he prepared himself a pot of coffee and sat down again at his desk to review the actions he planned to take against the embezzler. As he was bringing his coffee cup to his mouth, his hand paused in midair. The door to his outer office opened, and Eric walked into the room.

"I called Tyler this morning and he told me you would be here. Why in the world didn't you let me know you were back and have been for several days?" Eric halted in front of Steven's desk and slammed the folder he was carrying down on top of it. "I've been trying to reach you in Hawaii for the last few hours and even tried to get a hold of Lydia's number. But it was unlisted. Of course, I should have realized Tyler would know where you are sooner than I did."

Steven's brows furrowed as he placed his cup down with the same tightly controlled movements he had used the whole time he had been in New York. He felt as though he were an abused wind-up doll. "Is there a problem?"

"Problem? Well, if you call a fire at the plant in Germany a problem, then yes, there's a problem." Eric collapsed into the chair in front of the desk, the lines in his face carved deep by his exhaustion. "I've been on the phone most of the night with our German people. The fire destroyed almost all of the lab, the one we were just about through converting."

Why in the hell now? Steven wondered. He usually thrived on a challenge or a problem, but he was just too tired.

"Why wasn't Tyler informed when this happened? He knew exactly where I was." Steven said, taking his sip of coffee now. He figured during the next hours he would need a lot of coffee to keep himself going.

Eric's jaw set in a hard line and his eyes became slits. "Was this another time that you made me a figurehead without any real power?"

"No. We have a deal. You're the head of the European project."

"When I came back from Hawaii, I made it very clear everything on the European project would go through me. Tyler didn't argue. He has been preoccupied a lot lately. That's why the German foreman called me in the middle of the night to tell me.''

"Was anyone injured? How much was damaged?"

"Two people are in the hospital in fair condition, and the damage is extensive to the lab area, millions of dollars' worth. The insurance people want to meet with us at the site. I also think since so much is at stake here for Wintercom that both of us should look the plant over personally and see where we can best minimize the time loss. I've got the company plane ready and waiting." Eric rose and gathered up the folder he had thrown down earlier. "I've got all the information in here. You can look it over on the way to Munich."

"Hold it. Are you feeling well? Is this my brother talking?"

Eric was starting to turn away when he stopped and looked back at Steven. Suddenly he smiled, some of the tired lines about his eyes vanishing. "I know I sound crazy, but I need that twenty-five thousand dollars and this is the only way I can get it legally. Mother wouldn't lend me another cent either. I think that's what really did it. I expected you to tell me that someday, but not Mother." His smile grew. "Besides, you actually put me in charge of something. I like the power I feel and I like the feeling of accomplishment this European project has given me."

"Why do you need the twenty-five thousand dollars?"

Eric dropped his gaze to the floor and for a long moment he didn't say anything. Then looking directly into Steven's eyes, he answered, "I got drunk one night and got married to a woman I hardly knew. She'll take twenty-five thousand dollars to be rid of me as a husband."

It took all Steven's willpower not to laugh. His brother married! But quickly his thoughts sobered as he noticed the distress in Eric's features. Perhaps his brother was finally growing up. Steven decided that the trip to Germany would be a good test. If Eric could handle the crisis, he would give his brother more responsibility.

"We'll have to shift our priorities around and work out a new schedule," Eric said, turning toward the door.

"I have a few things I need to clear up here. I'll be able to leave at noon." As Eric was about to leave, Steven added, "Have you considered getting to know your wife and making a go of it?"

Eric laughed. "I met her in Atlantic City. She was looking for a rich husband and I was looking for a good time. Boy, this time I really outdid myself. I've discovered it's dangerous to my health to live too high. I'll have the limousine ready to take us to the airport at twelve."

When Eric closed the door behind him, Steven stared at it for a long time. A lot had happened since he had been gone and not all bad. Steven buzzed his secretary and asked her to locate Tyler and have him come to the office immediately. He wanted to settle one problem before he took on another.

It wasn't five minutes later that Tyler entered Steven's office. "Are you going to Germany?"

"Yes. In a few hours, but first I wanted you to know I found our man. It's Bruce."

"I was afraid of that."

"I haven't the time to take care of this personally. I need to wrap up a few things before heading back out of here, but I want you to confront our vice president of finance. I want all the money returned, and of course his chances of ever working in a top position again are ruined, but I won't press charges. I think by the time everything is over with he'll have paid dearly. I don't know how long I'll be in Germany, but I'll try to look over these reports that have come to my attention before I leave." He flicked his hand toward a small stack of papers.

"I never asked when you returned from Hawaii, but has everything been taken care of with Lydia Masters?"

"Everything taken care of?" Steven felt like laughing to relieve the tension. "Yes, if you mean my guilt over the accident. She took care of that."

"Are you going to pay any of her bills?"

"No. Take care of Bruce, Tyler, and I'll get back with you when I have a chance in Germany." Steven's tone clearly dismissed the subject of Lydia Masters.

After Tyler left, Steven read through the reports and jotted down some notes for the various department heads, then placed the few important calls he had to make. When he had finished with the immediate business at hand, he filled his briefcase with the papers he would need in Germany, then turned to the phone again to make his last call to Lydia.

"I hope I didn't awaken you, Lydia."

"No, you know me and sunrises. I was about to walk along the beach. Did you find your embezzler?"

"Yes and it wasn't Eric." Steven paused, inhaled a deep breath, then continued, "I have to leave in a few minutes for Europe."

"Is there a problem in Europe?"

Lydia's voice, full of concern, sounded so wonderful that Steven didn't ever want to end the conversation. But glancing at his watch, he noted he only had ten minutes. *Ten minutes and so much to say.* Would there ever be time for the little things in life like a conversation with someone who was special to you?

"Steven?"

"Oh, I'm sorry, Lydia. Yes, there's a problem. There's been a fire at a plant in Germany that's going to set our European expansion back at least a few months." Hesitating, Steven tried to find the right words to say what he felt was the only correct thing to do for Lydia's sake. "I don't know how long I'll be, Lydia. I . . ." His voice faltered. Then swallowing several times, he continued, "I'll be tied up with Wintercom for a while and I don't know when I'll get to see you again. There was a lot of work sitting on my desk for me to do and . . ." He stopped in mid-sentence. He was making up excuses because he was afraid to hurt Lydia again. He was afraid to ask her to wait because he didn't know if a few weeks or months would change things between them. "Lydia, I have to go. Eric is waiting. Good-bye."

"Good-bye, Steven," Lydia murmured, but all she heard was the dial tone. Her hand seemed to go numb and the receiver slipped from her grasp to thump on the carpet.

Good-bye. Good-bye. Good-bye! The finality of those words bombarded her with Steven's hidden message. She wouldn't hold him again. She wouldn't hear his voice again. She wouldn't see him again!

The air in the living room was stifling like a furnace,

and Lydia sought refuge in the cool dawn along the beach. She laboriously walked, using her cane, up and down the shore, her pace slow in the sand, her concentration totally focused on each step she took away from where Steven and she had shared so many wonderful moments.

Oblivious to the roar of the surf or to the bright vivid colors of a sunrise, Lydia didn't want a thought or a sensation to enter her mind. Lost in an empty abyss, she welcomed the relief.

Finally when her ankle protested with a dull ache, she stopped at the log under her pine tree and sat down to stare at the water. Slowly she once again became aware of the flight of a Mynah bird, the chirp of a cardinal, the relentless crash of the waves, the whisper of the palm fronds in the light caressing breeze.

Then the marauding thoughts returned; the succession of problems she had faced, the ones she still had to handle. But all that meant little to Lydia at the moment. Thoughts of Steven dominated her mind again. From the beginning she had known their timing had been all wrong and now she had to pay for ignoring her common sense and plunging into an affair with a man who had told her he couldn't promise her tomorrow. She wanted a tomorrow with him, a forever and always. But those were promises that Steven Winters wasn't capable of making.

Slowly tears filled her eyes, spilled over onto her cheeks, and burned a path down her face. She tasted the salt of her sorrow, knowing that people were beginning to come onto the beach and were staring at her. But she didn't care, because a special man had taught her not to be concerned about what strangers thought. And yet, he had been *her stranger* those first days on the beach and she had begun to feel again, to really care when she had thought all she could feel was anger and bitterness. He had shown her that she was more than a dancer and now that she could no longer dance that she would have to rely on the woman who was Lydia Masters.

The ache in her heart overrode any she felt in her ankle as she made her way toward the house. Out of the corner of her eye, she caught a glimpse of Steven's house and her loneliness intensified. She desperately wished that any second Steven would rush out onto the terrace, half dressed, late for his morning jog. She quickly diverted her gaze. The first day he had left she had made a mistake by wandering over there. The deserted house had echoed her empty feelings and she had avoided the place and grounds ever since. But she still found herself staring out the window at various times during the day as if she was waiting for him to appear on the beach.

Lydia sank back against the railing for support, her fingers digging into the redwood. She had to get out of here. She couldn't stay another day and be inundated with all her potent memories everywhere she turned. It was time to get on with her life.

"Lydia, are you all right?" Jason asked, stepping out onto the terrace.

The expression on his sister's face was one of pain and sorrow. Jason knew then that the phone call that morning had been from Steven and obviously the news had been bad. He had liked Steven that night he had met him, but he had also recognized a man who was wrestling with some questions that concerned himself.

"Lydia, I may have leaned on you a lot since Diana's death, but I've always been a good listener."

Her eyes misted with unshed tears. "I have to leave, Jason, today."

"Was that Steven on the phone earlier?"

"Yes, he has to fly to Europe for who knows how long."

"Lydia, when you run a corporation as large as Wintercom, you have more responsibilities than most people. He's been away a long time." Jason leaned against the railing next to Lydia, his eyes penetrating and perceptive.

"Europe isn't the problem. Steven told me good-bye. I believe he doesn't think he can handle a family and his job, too."

"You wanted to marry Steven?" Jason placed his hand over Lydia's and eased her fingers loose.

"Yes, and have children. Before I'd never had the time for either. Now I want both with Steven. I want a home like the one we grew up in. Mom and Dad were great with us."

"Where in the world did we go wrong?"

"We chose careers that demanded all of us and left little for anyone else. You've taken the first step by semi-retiring and trying to make a new home for Maggie."

"Yeah, but I'm a little too late for Diana."

"But not for Maggie. Pity, as I've learned, does no good. Pity destroys, Jason. Don't look at what could have been, but what can be."

A rueful slant to Jason's mouth teased her. "My little sister is just full of wisdom this morning."

"It was a hard lesson, but it finally sank in." Returning the playful grin, Lydia pushed herself away from the railing. "Now I have a lot to do starting with a call to the airlines for a reservation on the afternoon flight."

"Make that three reservations."

Lydia swung around at the glass door. "Three? But you two just got here."

"Maggie and I are going to visit Mom and Dad. You were right about our childhood. Maybe I'll get some pointers from them."

"You know, Jason, you've got a great idea. I think I'll make three reservations for Louisville."

"What are you going to do after we leave Louisville?" Jason followed Lydia into the house.

"I know all the things I don't want to do, but nothing I'm sure I want to do. There was a time that thought panicked me because I've always been so busy that I was scared of any free time I had. Now, though, I'm learning that time for oneself is important. I'm playing the piano again and experimenting a lot in the kitchen as well as reading all those books I never had time for."

Jason grinned, a proud look in his eyes. "You're amazing, Lydia, and I love you. You get our reservations while I see about Maggie and breakfast."

"I can fix breakfast."

Jason headed across the living room. "No, I know you like to do your exercises before breakfast. So go ahead and maybe Maggie will, too." Coming to a stop at the entrance into the hallway, he faced her. "Yesterday after you two did those dance movements, Maggie was more responsive than she had been since Diana's death. She hugged you, Lydia, and she spoke in more than one or two word sentences. And she went to the beach with us."

"But she just sat on the towel. She wouldn't swim or play in the surf. Don't get your hopes up too high, Jason."

"But don't you see she went out on her own accord and she did help a little with the sandcastle. Something you did triggered a response in Maggie," Jason replied vehemently.

"I have an idea, Jason, that might work, but I'm no therapist."

Lydia made her call to the airlines, then selected some music for her exercise routine. She was through with her warm-up when Maggie appeared in the doorway. With only a smile toward her niece but no words, Lydia flipped the stereo on and the sounds from a slow melody penetrated every corner of the room. Lydia began to dance to the music, swaying and moving slowly. Maggie was drawn into the room by the charismatic rhythm that pierced her wall of dammed emotions and allowed them to flow.

Then the tempo increased, the beat fast and wild. Maggie's feelings poured from her, her agitated body movements conveying the pent-up anger. She twisted, stretched, jumped, contorting her slim body into unusual positions. Her face was no longer devoid of expression but pinched into a look of rage, untamed, uninhibited.

Maggie sagged to the floor when the music swelled to

a loud thundering finish, the final clash of cymbals deafening. Lydia, who had stopped halfway through the dance, knelt beside her niece and gathered the child into her arms. Her hand stroked the length of Maggie's back as Lydia murmured soothing words of love.

"Aunt Lydia, Mommy's gone. She left me." Maggie's voice cracked and tears glistened in her eyes.

"She didn't want to, Maggie, but she left you with your daddy, who loves you very much."

"He left me, too." The tears streamed down Maggie's face, soaking Lydia's knit shirt.

"Adults sometimes make mistakes. Your daddy loved your mommy so much that it took a while for him to come to terms with her death. He was hurting so much that I don't think he realized anyone else was hurting like he was."

Maggie didn't say anything else but instead, drew in deep breaths, her tears ceasing. She pulled away from Lydia, wiping at her face with the back of her hand. Maggie's expression was again void of emotions, but for the first time Lydia felt with some patience that her niece would be all right.

Lydia stood and placed an arm about Maggie's slender shoulders. *Life goes on,* Lydia thought, *and you have to be prepared to go with it.*

Chapter Fourteen

Sheila Masters refilled the coffee cups, then placed the glass pot back on its stand. "First Jason and Maggie two days ago and now you have to leave. You've only been here a week, Lydia."

"But I'll return to Louisville soon. I have to take care of some things before I move back here," Lydia said, watching the steam rise from her coffee.

"Are you sure this is what you want?"

"Mom, I'm very sure and it feels wonderful. For months the uncertainty of my future has been hanging over my head. Now I know what I want to do." Lydia leaned forward, her palms flat on the kitchen table, and eagerly continued, "As I watched Maggie open up using dance movements to express her feelings, I saw a chance for me to use my knowledge of music and dance to work with children who are emotionally troubled. I told Jason I wasn't equipped to be a therapist, but after I go back to school, I intend to be."

Sheila frowned, a deep, thoughtful look in her eyes. "Do you think Maggie will be all right?" she asked after a long pause.

"Yes. You heard what Jason said last night. Their therapy session yesterday was their best one yet."

"Yes, but Maggie feels betrayed by Jason for not being there when Diana died."

"When feelings are expressed and out in the open, a person is better able to handle them. Maggie has been deeply hurt, but Jason loves his daughter. They need each other and I think Maggie is finally seeing that."

"Oh, Lydia, but the other morning when Jason came into the room to watch Maggie dance . . ." Sheila's eyes clouded.

Lydia recalled the anger in Maggie when her niece had flown at Jason and pounded her small fists into his chest, tears, for the second time since her mother's death, tumbling down her face. But Lydia also remembered Maggie finally calming down as Jason held his daughter tightly to him, telling her over and over that he loved her. That had been when Maggie had wrapped her arms about her father and hugged him fiercely.

"That's why Jason took Maggie back earlier than he had planned. Things were happening so quickly. I don't think anyone realized Maggie felt quite the way she did, but I think when Diana died so unexpectedly, Maggie felt totally alone, abandoned and frightened because she hadn't been around her father very much. Instead of helping each other, they pulled away and grieved in their own private hell."

Sheila finished the last swallow of her coffee, her

hand trembling as she brought the cup to her mouth. She stared beyond Lydia for a moment, then swung her attention abruptly back to her daughter. "This certainly has been a rough year for all of us." She placed her cup back on the table, her movements slow as if she were trying to gain control. "Your father will be home soon and we'll need to leave for the airport if you're going to make your flight."

Lydia looked pointedly at her mother. "The Masters clan is pulling through with flying colors. Jason and I will both be embarking on new careers. Dad is much better and Maggie will be soon."

Sheila laughed, relieving the tension. "If at this time last year anyone had told me that my son was thinking of buying a country inn and my daughter was going back to school to work with children who have emotional problems, I would have said he was crazy."

Smiling, Lydia rose and kissed her mother on the cheek. "It is a bit different from what we have been doing. Still, I'll be involved with dance and Jason intends to continue writing music for some of his friends in the business. But he wants to be around for Maggie and this way he can be." Lydia made her way toward the door. "I'd better pack. I know how nervous Dad gets if he doesn't have plenty of time to drive to the airport."

"Are you going to see Anthony while you're in New York?" Sheila asked, standing in the doorway of Lydia's old bedroom, everything the same as it had been since she was a teenager.

Lydia's gaze strayed to her first pair of toe shoes hanging up on the wall. A lump formed in her throat at the memory of her first time dancing on point before an audience. She had some beautiful memories that would always be with her, ones of her dancing and ones of her with Steven. But she wasn't sure she would be able to see Anthony at the studio. Maybe on neutral territory, Lydia thought as she turned toward her mother. Anthony and the dance world, however, weren't her main reasons for leaving New York. As big as the city was, it wasn't big enough if there was even the slightest chance she would see Steven or read about him. That she knew she couldn't handle.

"I don't know," Lydia finally answered.

"You can't leave New York without saying good-bye to Anthony. He's done so much for you."

"I know. I'll at least talk with him on the phone."

Lydia sat in the viewing booth two days later, still wondering how in the world she had let Anthony talk her into coming to the studio to see everybody.

The company was between seasons, but the dancers still took morning classes even though they weren't performing at night. Lydia was thankful no one else was watching the dancers, and earlier she had refused Anthony's suggestion to view the class from downstairs in the studio. Now that she was on the outside looking in, she wanted to be alone until she was used to the idea.

As the company members finished their barre exercises, Lydia's palms were sweaty. Wiping them on her jeans, she kept her gaze trained on the dancers, some of whom had been like a family to her for years. They looked good. Lydia had heard the spring season had gone well.

For a fleeting moment as Dora did a series of

pirouettes across the floor, jealousy overpowered everything else. Then as suddenly as the feeling appeared, it vanished. A resigned sense of peace overcame Lydia. She would be a student again, learning a new craft. There were a lot of children like Maggie who could use a form of art for self-expression, using dance movements to convey their troubled emotions better than words. Hadn't she always been able to express herself better through her dancing. Until Steven had entered her life she had understood, and still did, what it had been like to have so many intense feelings bottled up inside of her and at times no way to express them adequately, except through dance.

Steven. Everything always came back to him. Would he solve his problem in Europe? Yes, she was sure he would if he hadn't already. Then there would be another problem for him. He was a problem solver, thriving on challenges. Perhaps that was why she had so intrigued him in the first place. She had definitely challenged his sense to conquer, to control.

Lydia quickly pushed her thoughts away from the subject of Steven. Her fragile, hard-earned peace was threatened with thoughts of him. Again she focused her full attention on the dancers below. The ninety-minute class was coming to an end and it was time she made her way downstairs to say hello to everyone.

Bolstering herself with several deep breaths, she descended the stairs to the studio, no longer aided by her cane. It had been a long battle, but now she had complete mobility. Only when she did too much would her ankle swell or throb, reminding her of the accident. Outwardly she was healed; inwardly she was mending, as much as possible without the man she loved.

Immediately Lydia was besieged by friends, everyone hugging her and kissing her until she felt like a bean bag being tossed around a circle. After a few minutes, she held up both of her hands. "Hey, hold it. Don't you know I'm fragile. I've been recuperating for the last few months." Lydia's teasing tone released any restraints the dancers around her might have had.

"Yeah, lying around on a beach in sunny Hawaii. We feel for you, Lydia," a male dancer quipped.

"We've been slaving away while you've been relaxing," Dora added, "and here I needed your help with a role that I'll be dancing during the fall season."

Everyone began to talk at once, wanting her opinion about a ballet or her advice concerning a new toe shoe on the market. Quickly Lydia found herself submersed into the camaraderie that she had enjoyed as a member of the company. She would miss it, she realized suddenly, her smile fading slightly as a bittersweet feeling assailed her.

"Okay, everyone give her room to breathe." Anthony pushed his way through the crowd, giving the company members his stern expression of authority that in class or rehearsal commanded their immediate attention. "I want to have a few words with Lydia. She'll see you in a moment."

"A few words!" Someone laughed, joined by others.

"A minute? Did we hear you correctly?" another dancer chimed in.

"Come on, Anthony. We all know how long-winded you can be," Dora said, giving Lydia a quick hug. "Come back again and say hello to us. We'll probably all be long gone by the time you emerge from Anthony's office after one of his *little* talks."

The company members said their good-byes, telling Lydia not to be a stranger before they headed for their dressing rooms. Lydia watched them walk away, knowing this would be the last time she saw them for a long time. Tears blurred her vision and she quickly blinked them away. She still had Anthony to deal with.

In a few minutes the hall was cleared and she was left alone with the director. She glanced around her at the long passageway with doors leading to several studios and the dressing rooms for the dancers. This place was more familiar to her than her own apartment. A good part of her life had been spent here, she reflected. Her throat closed at the thought she was going from the familiar to the unknown.

"Let's go into the studio instead of my office." Anthony's voice broke into Lydia's thoughts.

Lydia hesitated. She knew full well what Anthony was up to. "It's not going to work. I already have plans for my future."

"At least give me a chance to say the pitch I've rehearsed all day."

"It's only eleven thirty," she retorted lightly.

"Well, then part of the day," he countered.

"Then will you leave me alone about the ballet mistress position?" Her voice rang with desperation.

His shoulders sagged forward. "Yes. If you persist in being stubborn, then I'll have to relent and admit defeat. But, Lydia, my dear, that's a hard word for me to swallow."

"I know," she murmured, placing her hand on his arm. "We've been friends for a long time."

He slipped his arm about her waist. "Come on into the studio and tell me about this future you've planned for yourself. Is it truly what you want, Lydia? I see a deep sadness in your eyes."

Anthony walked with her into the studio and they sat on the piano bench, her hand comfortably settled within his grasp. Lydia stared for a long moment at the dance floor. So much of her life had occurred in this room. Sweat. Toil. Tears. Elation. Exhilaration. Words flitted through her mind, all sparking memories of her long fight to the top.

The intense urge to dance made her squeeze her eyes tightly shut to block the image of the studio from her mind. It didn't work. She knew every inch of the room, having floated, leaped, twirled, sailed over the hardwood floor through the years. She suffocated with the memories, her breathing shallow gasps, her heart beating so slowly she thought it would stop at any second.

"Will you dance with me, Anthony?"

"Dance?"

Surprise laced his voice, and Lydia opened her eyes and turned them to his puzzling expression. "For old time's sake. One last dance, Anthony, before I walk away from the only life I've known." She laid her other hand over their clasped ones. "Don't you see when I do something I throw everything I have into it. It's all or nothing with me, Anthony."

Anthony looked deeply into her eyes for a full minute, then rose and pulled her to her feet. Lydia kicked off her shoes and danced in her bare feet. For a brief span of time they moved together, the steps never complicated or demanding but a continuous graceful flow as though they were a gentle rippling stream.

By the time the soft love ballad Anthony had put on the stereo ended, tears were cascading down Lydia's face. This had been her home for so long that it would be hell to walk away. She knew herself well, though; she had given herself to dance wholly, and she would never be able to teach ballet and not wish she were the student.

Anthony drew her into his arms and silently comforted her. "I'm sorry for the pain," he said after a while, when the tears had subsided. "I'm sorry I pressured you. I forgot for a brief time the woman I've known for so long. Just remember you will always have a home here." He gazed down at her, a deep friendship in his eyes. "Tell me what your plans are."

Lydia touched his face, a tightness choking her words. In a hoarse whisper she said, "I know you care. Thank you, Anthony."

"For what?"

He was dangerously close to becoming emotional, Lydia could tell, and sought to lighten the mood. "For being the same opinionated, stubborn"—she smiled— "and lovable man who insisted I dance *Swan Lake* before I was ready."

"You were ready. You just hadn't realized it yet. Come on. I'll walk you outside. Didn't you tell me you had some packing to do and couldn't spare much time? Something about a plane to catch."

The minute Lydia had stepped off the plane in New York two days before, she had known she couldn't stay. New York now belonged to Steven and the pain of being so near, yet a world apart, ripped her in two. No, she couldn't stay any longer than it was necessary to pack and make arrangements to move.

"That's not until the day after tomorrow. But I still do have a lot of packing."

"Well, Lydia Masters, what are you going to do with the rest of your life?"

With his arm about her shoulder, Lydia and Anthony left the studio. "I'm going back to school. I want to work with emotionally troubled children. I want to use my dancing as a tool to draw them out."

"You'll be good at that, Lydia. I know how much you love children. I've seen you at the benefits we've danced, especially the ones for the hospitals. You've always been drawn to the young ones."

Yes, she loved children and wanted a family of her own—with Steven. *But that's not possible,* she reminded herself as they made their way to the street level.

Anthony lifted his hand and signaled for a taxi. A cab stopped immediately and they both exchanged stunned looks, then laughed.

"Of course, that would never happen if I'd been in a hurry." Merriment lit her eyes as she brushed her lips over Anthony's. "I'll keep in touch."

"No, you won't. You'll become so absorbed in your new life I won't hear from you except perhaps at Christmas and on my birthday."

"I'm a lousy letter writer, but I'll call. I may be moving on, Anthony, but I won't forget. I couldn't. Not all the years." The tears in her throat had returned. She quickly kissed her old partner and friend, slid into the back seat of the taxi, and raised a hand in farewell as the cab pulled away from the curb.

The tears flowed as she gave the driver her address. Damn! Why was she being so emotional? She had made the decision to cut all her ties with the dance world and New York. But the good-byes hurt so much.

She rubbed at the tears that continued to fall. *Like a blasted faucet that I can't turn off*, she thought as the taxi passed by familiar scenery.

I could go to college in New York. I could . . .

No! She wouldn't, and couldn't, hang around in hopes of catching a glimpse of Steven. He already carried enough guilt around with him; she wouldn't be a constant reminder wherever he turned. She had set him free completely in Hawaii and she wouldn't chain him to her again out of guilt or pity.

The cab screeched to a stop outside her apartment building. Sighing deeply, Lydia erased the last of her tears and fumbled in her purse for the fare.

By the time she had reached her apartment and was withdrawing her keys, she was tired from the long walk up four flights of stairs and from the emotional roller coaster she had been on the past few hours—past few months!

Once inside, she dropped her purse on the coffee table and turned slowly around, surveying the disarray of stacked boxes, scattered clothes and memorabilia of her years of traveling, years of dancing. So much to pack. She sank down onto the couch, picking up a faded program from her first performance as a soloist. Her name stood out in bold black letters, and she lovingly fingered the tattered page. She wouldn't forget her role as the fairy queen; it was carved into her thoughts like all her other memories. Some sad. Some happy. But all treasured, she decided, and laid the program in the box at her feet.

A knock at her front door forced a gasp from her lips. She wasn't expecting anyone; she didn't want to see anyone.

Wearily she crossed the living room and looked through the peephole. Without opening the door, she asked, "What do you want?"

"I have a delivery for Miss Lydia Masters."

"A delivery? I didn't order anything."

"Nevertheless, I have some—chocolate letters for you."

"Chocolate letters?" Lydia threw open the door, her usual caution gone. Automatically she asked, "Who are they from?" That was a silly question. Her face glowed with a smile. No one sent her chocolate except Steven.

"There wasn't a name on the delivery form."

"That's okay." She waved the ridiculous question away. "Where are they?"

"Right here." The delivery man indicated a second man positioned down the hall as they both bent and lifted a six foot long slab of wood with one foot high chocolate letters that spelled out, "I love you, Lydia."

Even her name! Boy, she was going to have a field day with his message. At least ten pounds of love, sculpted in delicious, mouth-watering chocolate, she decided as she gestured for the men to place the message in her living room and scanned the hallway for Steven. Surely he wouldn't send her this message and not come also. But the hallway was empty.

After the delivery men left, shaking their heads in amusement, Lydia sat again on the couch and stared at the huge brown letters that dwarfed her small living room. Maybe she should eat one letter a day. No, it would take at least a week. And savor each bite of chocolate, she thought with wonderful anticipation.

The next knock when it came sent her flying across the room, her ankle objecting to the abuse so soon. She flung the door open and was ready to throw herself into Steven's arms. But the scowl on his face arrested her movements.

"Did you even look to see who it was?" he asked, the scowl softening a bit at her bewilderment.

She smiled then. "I knew it was you. Who else would it be after that wonderfully ridiculous message you just sent me?"

"But what if it hadn't been?" Steven persisted, stepping into her apartment and closing the door behind him.

"Steven! Are we going to fight about something as silly as my opening the door without checking first."

"Yes, if that makes you cautious the next time." Steven's scowl was completely gone, and he gathered her into the circle of his arms. "Oh, how I've missed the smell of you," he breathed deeply, "the feel of you," he touched her face with a finger, "and the taste of you," he took her mouth in a deep, soul-searching kiss.

Lydia felt lost. In Steven's embrace she couldn't think straight. She would always be his, no matter what. But she wanted all of him and was willing to take a gamble.

With extreme willpower that she was amazed she possessed at the moment, Lydia pulled away and placed a few feet between them in order to calm her rapidly beating heart. "Did you mean this?" she asked, indicating the chocolate message.

"Every delicious word." Steven moved to take her back into his embrace.

She halted his movements with a probing look. "Are you sure, Steven? I have to have all of you. Not just bits and pieces from time to time."

"Very sure." His simple declaration filled the small space between them.

But Lydia continued to resist. With her hands on her hips, she defiantly asked, "And just what are you going to do about it?"

One corner of his mouth lifted in a crooked grin that beguiled Lydia and almost sent her falling forward into his arms.

"I'm going to help you eat those chocolate letters. It will probably take us at least our entire honeymoon. What do you think?" Steven stood perfectly still with his arms straight at his sides, making no attempt to take Lydia into his embrace.

"Honeymoon?" Lydia replied almost dazed. "Is this an offhanded way to ask me to marry you?"

"I'll get down on my knee if that's what it'll take for you to say yes. Lydia," he began, then swearing softly, covered the distance between them and pulled her close to his heart. "Ah, now that's much better. I feel half naked without you here next to me."

Lydia nestled even closer, gazing up at him saucily. "What's so bad about that. I kind of like you half naked." Toying with his top button, she unfastened it. "Or, for that matter, completely naked isn't too bad either."

With a silver gleam in his eyes, Steven held her fingers still. "Let's clear up the merger first before we take a pleasure cruise."

"When do I sign the papers?"

"As soon as I can get the license."

"No big production for our family and friends?"

His strong hands captured her face. "Do you mind?"

"No."

"Good." Steven grinned, kissing the tip of her nose. "Instead, after our honeymoon we'll throw the biggest party that this town has ever seen."

His lips came down upon hers in fiery devotion, his tongue sweeping into her mouth with a demanding need. Then he scooped her up into his arms and cradled her close, burying his face into her mass of hair. "Mmm. I've missed carrying you." Glancing around for the first time, he added, "One thing about small apartments is that you have little choice on which way is the bedroom." He headed for his only choice.

Steven stood her next to the bed, his hands on her shoulders. "I love you, Lydia. I don't want to spend the rest of my life alone. I want you. I want a family."

"How about two or three?"

"Two or three, what?"

"Children, silly." She laughed at him, her world bright and wonderful. At this moment she felt as if she could dance on air.

"I talked with your mother this morning and she told me what you plan on doing. Will you be able to do both?"

"I'm like you, Steven. I thrive on work, but only to a point now. I want to return to school, but my family will always come first. I've spent all my youth and adult years working hard at a career. Now, I want a husband and children."

"In New York City with millions of people around me I was more alone than on Kauai where we only saw a few people."

"You aren't alone anymore." Lydia wound her arms around his neck and fitted herself against his sinewy planes. "And, Mr. Winters, if you dare start working too much, I'll kidnap you and whisk you away to a deserted beach along the Na Pali Coast."

Amusement glittered in his eyes. "I think you mean that."

"You'd better believe it." Lydia shoved Steven back onto her bed. "Now, that's enough talk. Let's cement this merger."

Lydia was beside him on the bed, completing her earlier task of unbuttoning his shirt, then spreading her fingers wide and moving them over his chest in tantalizing circles. He shuddered beneath her hands, and she was excited at the thought of what she could do to him.

"Oh, you feel wonderful," she murmured against his ear, planting tiny kisses on the lobe as she spoke.

Then everything moved with an urgency. They hurriedly undressed, each fumbling and laughing at the other's eagerness. The time for leisurely pleasure was for later. Instead, Steven rediscovered the hypersensitive areas of her body, exploring every inch with fingers that heated her to a white-hot readiness. Their union was a wild mating that spoke of long suppressed needs and wants.

Afterward, they lay side by side, their lengths pressed together. Their ragged breathing mingled with the quiet of the apartment, bringing a calm tranquility to Lydia.

Her life had changed drastically since the accident and would continue to change, but she had found a new home, a new purpose to her life. Steven had given her a tomorrow, filled with a promise of a full life.

Turning in toward Steven, she smiled, warmed from the glow of their lovemaking. Lydia tangled her fingers in the hair on his chest. "Steven, when you called me the last time in Kauai, you were saying good-bye for good, weren't you?"

He gathered her nearer to him, as though to fuse her to his body. "Yes. I've been known to do a few foolish things before. Not many, mind you."

Laughing, Lydia asked, "What changed your mind?"

"My business trip to Europe. Nothing's been the same since I came back from Hawaii. I really suppose it hasn't been the same for a long time, but meeting you and falling in love with you made me see it. I took a good hard look at my life and saw I really had nothing of worth." He smiled with dry humor. "Do you realize that I was so efficient at my job that Wintercom can survive on occasion without my presence."

"But will you be able to slow down? Will you be able to survive without Wintercom?" Lydia turned over onto her stomach and raised herself up on her elbows, resting her chin in the palms of her hands.

"I have to. My little brother is demanding a greater say in Wintercom." His eyes shone with pride. "You should have seen Eric in Germany. I knew my brother was intelligent and capable, but I think he even amazed himself. It's about time I hand over some of the corporation's management to him. After all, he's the young man in the family."

"Well, come here, old man, and kiss me," Lydia murmured in a sultry voice.

Silhouette Special Edition. Romances
for the woman who expects a little
more out of love.

If you enjoyed this book, and you're ready for more great romance

...get 4 romance novels FREE when you become a Silhouette Special Edition home subscriber.

Act now and we'll send you four exciting Silhouette Special Edition romance novels. They're our gift to introduce you to our convenient home subscription service. Every month, we'll send you six new passion-filled Special Edition books. Look them over for 15 days. If you keep them, pay just $11.70 for all six. Or return them at no charge.

We'll mail your books to you two full months *before they are available anywhere else.* Plus, with every shipment, you'll receive the Silhouette Books Newsletter absolutely free. *And with Silhouette Special Edition there are never any shipping or handling charges.*

Mail the coupon today to get your four free books—and more romance than you ever bargained for.

Silhouette Special Edition

MORE ROMANCE FOR
A SPECIAL WAY TO RELAX

$2.25 each

79 ☐ Hastings	105 ☐ Sinclair	131 ☐ Lee	157 ☐ Taylor
80 ☐ Douglass	106 ☐ John	132 ☐ Dailey	158 ☐ Charles
81 ☐ Thornton	107 ☐ Ross	133 ☐ Douglass	159 ☐ Camp
82 ☐ McKenna	108 ☐ Stephens	134 ☐ Ripy	160 ☐ Wisdom
83 ☐ Major	109 ☐ Beckman	135 ☐ Seger	161 ☐ Stanford
84 ☐ Stephens	110 ☐ Browning	136 ☐ Scott	162 ☐ Roberts
85 ☐ Beckman	111 ☐ Thorne	137 ☐ Parker	163 ☐ Halston
86 ☐ Halston	112 ☐ Belmont	138 ☐ Thornton	164 ☐ Ripy
87 ☐ Dixon	113 ☐ Camp	139 ☐ Halston	165 ☐ Lee
88 ☐ Saxon	114 ☐ Ripy	140 ☐ Sinclair	166 ☐ John
89 ☐ Meriwether	115 ☐ Halston	141 ☐ Saxon	167 ☐ Hurley
90 ☐ Justin	116 ☐ Roberts	142 ☐ Bergen	168 ☐ Thornton
91 ☐ Stanford	117 ☐ Converse	143 ☐ Bright	169 ☐ Beckman
92 ☐ Hamilton	118 ☐ Jackson	144 ☐ Meriwether	170 ☐ Paige
93 ☐ Lacey	119 ☐ Langan	145 ☐ Wallace	171 ☐ Gray
94 ☐ Barrie	120 ☐ Dixon	146 ☐ Thornton	172 ☐ Hamilton
95 ☐ Doyle	121 ☐ Shaw	147 ☐ Dalton	173 ☐ Belmont
96 ☐ Baxter	122 ☐ Walker	148 ☐ Gordon	174 ☐ Dixon
97 ☐ Shaw	123 ☐ Douglass	149 ☐ Claire	175 ☐ Roberts
98 ☐ Hurley	124 ☐ Mikels	150 ☐ Dailey	176 ☐ Walker
99 ☐ Dixon	125 ☐ Cates	151 ☐ Shaw	177 ☐ Howard
100 ☐ Roberts	126 ☐ Wildman	152 ☐ Adams	178 ☐ Bishop
101 ☐ Bergen	127 ☐ Taylor	153 ☐ Sinclair	179 ☐ Meriwether
102 ☐ Wallace	128 ☐ Macomber	154 ☐ Malek	180 ☐ Jackson
103 ☐ Taylor	129 ☐ Rowe	155 ☐ Lacey	181 ☐ Browning
104 ☐ Wallace	130 ☐ Carr	156 ☐ Hastings	182 ☐ Thornton

Silhouette Special Edition

$2.25 each

183 ☐ Sinclair	190 ☐ Wisdom	197 ☐ Lind	204 ☐ Eagle
184 ☐ Daniels	191 ☐ Hardy	198 ☐ Bishop	205 ☐ Browning
185 ☐ Gordon	192 ☐ Taylor	199 ☐ Roberts	206 ☐ Hamilton
186 ☐ Scott	193 ☐ John	200 ☐ Milan	207 ☐ Roszel
187 ☐ Stanford	194 ☐ Jackson	201 ☐ Dalton	208 ☐ Sinclair
188 ☐ Lacey	195 ☐ Griffin	202 ☐ Thornton	209 ☐ Ripy
189 ☐ Ripy	196 ☐ Cates	203 ☐ Parker	210 ☐ Stanford

SILHOUETTE SPECIAL EDITION, Department SE/2
1230 Avenue of the Americas
New York, NY 10020

Please send me the books I have checked above. I am enclosing $_____
(please add 75¢ to cover postage and handling. NYS and NYC residents please
add appropriate sales tax). Send check or money order—no cash or C.O.D.'s
please. Allow six weeks for delivery.

NAME _____

ADDRESS _____

CITY _____ STATE/ZIP _____

Silhouette Special Edition